Books by Kerry Hotaling

What They Endured, What they Wrought:
Comparing Regimental Casualties
at the Battle of Gettysburg

The Yankees Had Something to do with It

Go Forward Into the Storm

GO FORWARD INTO THE STORM

AN IWO JIMA JOURNAL

KERRY HOTALING

TO: TARA

WITH WARMEST REGARDS

K. Ht

2016

Christopher Matthews Publishing

www.christophermatthewspub.com

Boston, Massachusetts

Go Forward Into the Storm

Editors: Jeremy Soldevilla, Kevin Hotaling
Cover design: Neil Noah
Iwo Jima Map: Dan Delmonte
Photos are from Gage Hotaling's private collection

ISBN 9781938985911
ebook ISBN 9781938985928

Published by

CHRISTOPHER MATTHEWS PUBLISHING
www.christophermatthewspub.com
Boston

This book is dedicated to those whom Tom Brokaw called "The Greatest Generation"—the men and women who unselfishly risked their all so tyranny would not rule

ACKNOWLEDGMENTS

Our family was extremely fortunate during World War II. My grandparents, Emery and Gertrude Bauer, had six children. Four of their children served in combat along with the husband of their eldest daughter Adell Bauer Hotaling. All five returned.

They raised their families, and all experienced the joy of seeing many grandchildren born. They were the generation Tom Brokaw named, "The Greatest Generation." In their formative years they experienced the Great Depression, and when tyranny challenged the world order, they volunteered in record numbers to defeat it. They did not fight to conquer territory or to subjugate people. They fought for human dignity and to beat back oppressive regimes.

This book is about the life of one member of this generation and his time on Iwo Jima. Reverend E. Gage Hotaling was on Iwo Jima as a chaplain with the Fourth Marine Division. He buried 1800 young men on the island— young men whose families were not as fortunate as his. They died on an island they had never heard of before, fighting against an enemy that was entrenched underground. Fighting against an enemy that had brutalized conquered peoples across Asia since the late 1930's. Fighting against a formidable foe.

Parts of this diary were previously published in the magazine, *World War II Quarterly, 2013 Summer Edition.* The story was entitled "Doing God's Work in Hell." This book takes the words found in Gage Hotaling's journal and puts them into a story form. A story you will find most compelling and moving.

I wish to extend my thanks to my publisher Christopher Matthews Publishing and its editor Jeremy Soldevilla for having an interest in this book. He is always a pleasure to work with bringing a book to life.

I would also like to thank Dan Delmonte for his rendering of the map of Iwo Jima.

Most of the names in this book are actual people. There are a few exceptions I would like to list. The chaplain named Samuels is a fictitious name, but based on a person Gage met. The two marines named Decker and Gleason are also fictitious characters. Their names were picked at random by the author.

The letters at the end of the book were actual letters written by Gage during his time in the service. The names were intentionally omitted by the author so as not to cause any undue grief to any descendants.

The Greatest Generation gave their youth, blood and innocence so we could live in a free world. This book is my thanks to all from that generation and a gift to all who follow.

—Kerry Hotaling

A MOST FITTING TRIBUTE

The idea for this story came to me while on vacation in Florida during the winter of 2015. Getting out of the extremely cold Northeast for a few days seemed to thaw the brain enough for creative energies to flow through. I had no clue how I was going to write the story, just that this story needed to be told.

I began writing when I returned home and the style took on a life of its own. There was some other worldly inspiration going on while I put words down on paper, of that I am sure. I was brought to tears while writing parts of this book, and my group of proof readers told me they were bought to tears while reading it.

So, what is this book about? A young minister with a wife and young child signed up to be a Navy chaplain during World War II. He was expecting an assignment at a naval base; however, the Navy and God had other plans. From *Proverbs 16:9* we find these words. "A man's heart deviseth his way; but the Lord directs his steps." Instead of being assigned shore duty or duty on board a ship, he was assigned to the Marines and ended up on Iwo Jima. He spent 26 days on that island during the most ferocious battle the Marine Corps ever fought in World War II.

This young minister was my father, Reverend E. Gage Hotaling whose time on that island is chronicled for you in this book. Interwoven with the battle is the story of his early years as a minister and his special calling to the ministry. This story comes from his own words, the words found in his diaries, journals and letters home from overseas.

What is this most fitting tribute of which I speak? You will have to read the story to find out. Does God still have a hand in the affairs of this world? You won't get any argument from me when you discover the tribute bestowed upon Gage Hotaling fifty-five years after the battle.

I wish to humbly thank the readers of this manuscript as it was coming to life for their time in reading it and offering suggestions to make it a far better book than it would be without their input. The list includes Dan, Carol, Walter, Pam, John, Kathie, Tom and Kevin. It was their feedback that kept me writing and their encouragement that saw this project through.

As with my first book, *The Yankees Had Something to do With It*, my son Kevin read this with an editor's eye, finding all the errors and helping make it better. You have my deepest gratitude, Kevin. A cigar and a beer will come your way!

Table of Contents

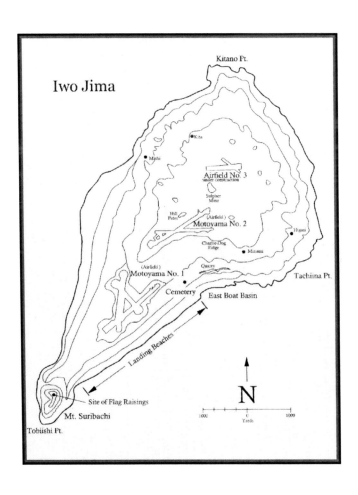

Iwo Jima

Kitano Pt.

Kita

Minbi

Airfield No. 3
under construction

Sulphur
Mine

Hill
Peter

(Airfield)
Motoyama No. 2

Higasi

Charlie-Dog
Ridge

Minami

Quarry

(Airfield)
Motoyama No. 1

Tachiina Pt.

Cemetery

East Boat Basin

Landing Beaches

N

Site of Flag Raisings

1000   0   1000
Yards

Mt. Suribachi

Tobiishi Pt.

FEBRUARY 21, 1945

THE ISLAND HAD BEEN UNDER CONSTANT bombardment for seventy-four days. The Navy had left no portion of the land untouched, blanketing the island with first air and then sea power. He was not sure how anything had survived. But the Japanese had survived and were fighting back with a sustained fury.

He was scheduled to go ashore on D-Day Plus 1, but the beaches had not been secured. Casualties for the Marines had been extremely heavy. It was now D Plus 2. The Higgins boat he was on pitched and rolled over the high seas. A woozy feeling settled in his stomach. He prayed not to lose his breakfast, as some did. He could hear the shelling, even over the drone of the motor and the turbulent ocean slapping under the boat.

The beach was partially secure, but the fighting was far from over. The orders had come down for his unit to get to shore. There was a job to do, even if it meant landing in the middle of a beach under a barrage of enemy fire.

He was Reverend Gage Hotaling, assigned to the Graves Registration section with the Fourth Marine Division. The Higgins boat tossing him around was headed for a tiny island called Iwo Jima. Just another island no one back home had ever heard of.

Gage was having quite the conversation with God and getting no response. Why was he in this place? He had signed up to be a chaplain in the Navy, yet here he was landing with the Marines in combat. His first born son Bill was eleven months old, and he would like to see him grow up.

Gage's mind drifted back to one particular day in Naval Chaplain School in Williamsburg, Virginia. He was the shortest person in his class. One of his classmates asked the instructor if any of them would be assigned to the Marines. The instructor told Gage to stand and said, "Some of you may be headed for the Marines, but Hotaling won't be one. He's too small!" Gage was the only member of his class assigned to the Marines. God certainly has a sense of humor.

Gage thought about the day he got his assignment. From his observations of other classes, it seemed the big husky fellows went to the Marines, so he felt reasonably sure he would get assigned to a Naval Station somewhere on the West Coast.

The executive officer was reading off names alphabetically and got to his. "Hotaling. Headquarters, Fleet Marine Force, Pacific." One could have knocked him over with a feather. He was stunned. His classmates congratulated him, for he would be the first one to draw overseas pay.

"Stack all gear in the corner. We are landing near the fuel dump and picking up casualties." He was jolted back to the present by orders being given. The fuel dump was burning fiercely.

Yea, tho I walk thru the valley of the shadow of death, I will fear no evil, for thou art with me.

The coxswain landed the boat, but they were about 150 yards from the burning dump.

Gage left the boat with the others, ran ashore and looked around for casualties. There were none to be found. No one seemed to know anything about casualties that were to be picked up at this location.

"Try further down the beach," someone yelled. "There are plenty of casualties."

"Incoming! Take cover!" came a shout.

Gage dove into a hole and felt the ground shake from the explosion. *That was too close! What am I doing here! This was no secure beachhead.*

There was a job to do. He got up out of the foxhole to see if he could find someone in charge. There was no order, only chaos. The sounds of gunfire, artillery and voices screaming filled the air.

"Corpsman!"

"We've gotta move inland!"

"Where's the captain?"

"Incoming!"

Again an artillery round was heard approaching. Men scurried for cover. The explosion was not as close as the last.

No one had any idea where the casualties they were ordered to pick up were, except that they weren't on this section of beach.

Gage turned to run back to the boat. Perhaps they landed on the wrong beach. What he saw stunned him. The boat was leaving. All his gear was still on board.

SEPTEMBER 1940

H IS FIRST CHURCH out of seminary was The Second Baptist Church in Palmer, Massachusetts. Gage and his young bride Adell (who was known as Dell) were young and energetic. He was having the time of his life getting things organized and making plans for his new church.

It was not his first choice in life to be a Baptist minister. He was at Brown University, studying history and education. He wished to be a history teacher or professor. Studying history was his passion. But God had other plans.

Gage's father was a minister and Gage was the only child of Ira and Albertha Hotaling. While a junior at Brown, Gage got the news that his dad was sick and did not have long to live. He was jolted by the news. His dad was in the prime of life, only 57 years old, and there was still work for him to do.

Gage was out walking on the campus on a crisp fall evening. The sun was sinking behind the horizon, lighting up the western sky in a brilliant orange hue. The colors were magnificent, but he could not see them. His mind was devoid of happiness. He was angry with God. Why strike down a man in the prime of life, a man who had so much to give to the world?

Did he hear a voice? He wasn't sure. Was he imagining? He wasn't sure. Was it real? He felt or thought he heard a message. "You are to carry on your father's work."

He looked around. There was no one near him. His father was a minister. Gage had never considered this path for work. He believed God chose you to be a minister . . . what was that voice he heard? He wondered.

The gnawing inside would not go away. The message was too strong to be coincidence. Was this his calling? Was this how God called people to do his work? The more he pondered, the more sure he became. Gage realized this was his calling into the ministry. He was to complete his father's work.

He went home to speak with his father. Ira was in his study. Gage always enjoyed going into this room. There was a huge roll top desk that was always open. There were papers neatly stacked on the flat surface that rested above two drawers on each side. There was an opening in the middle for a chair. The room also contained bookshelves filled with books on religion, history and biographies. Gage was a voracious reader and he had devoured many of the books in this office.

Now he was there for a different reason. His father was in his chair, working. When Gage entered, Ira put down the book he was reading.

"This is a surprise visit. What brings you here this time of day?" Ira asked.

"I've had an epiphany, Dad. God is beckoning me to be a minister," replied Gage.

Gage went on to tell his father of the recent events. He told him of the inner voice that would not go away and the tugging on his soul that persisted, until he understood the meaning.

Gage was frightened by the call, but he felt it now to be his life's vocation.

Ira's eyes filled with joy. His face became radiant. They sat for two hours discussing the preparation necessary for the ministry. It was a talk Gage would never forget.

Yes, Gage thought. I will carry on and finish Dad's work.

Ira's body was wracked in pain, but Gage was able to give his father this moment of happiness.

FEBRUARY 21, 1945

T HE BOAT WAS GONE, as was all his gear. The beach
was a scene of chaos and carnage. Two amtracs lay in a
heap, having been blown up. Wrecked landing craft
littered the beaches. There was twisted metal
everywhere. Vehicles were bogged down, having difficulty
moving through the sand. That awful volcanic sand—worst
stuff he had ever seen. It was like walking through a foot of
new fallen snow.

He darted from one shell hole to another, trying to calm
his nerves. One hole was as safe as the next, but he felt a need
to move. His nerves were on full throttle overdrive.

Lord, help me get through this day, he thought.

In one hole he found a can of C-rations and sat down and
ate them.

Enemy shelling was still finding the beach intermittently.
The Marines had pushed the enemy back a few hundred
yards, so the front lines were inland. This is where a vast
majority of the shelling was coming down. Still, some shells
came down on the beach, which put Gage in peril.

Since they had no gear, he and his boat mates determined to scrounge around the beach, looking for discarded supplies that could be useful to them. Gage was told to secure as many ponchos as he could. He had run track in school, but this sand was tiring to navigate. It was like running in a wheat bin.

Abandoned gear was strewn across the sand. He rummaged through it, seizing any ponchos he could find. Then he came upon a dead Marine.

Gage had performed funerals and seen bodies all fixed up in caskets. That was a clean, homogenized death. This was a harsh, violent death. Gage said a quick prayer for the Marine's soul, then took his poncho.

He ran as fast as he could to a shell hole away from the dead Marine. His thoughts were relentless. He had stolen from a dead Marine. Was he breaking any of God's laws? Had he committed an action that went against some moral code? There were no answers, only the haze of combat.

FALL 1940

THERE WAS PLENT Y OF WORK to be done in the new church. A Sunday evening service was added, and attendance was increasing for this each week. A Young People's Fellowship club for teens had started with thirteen people, and within just five weeks the attendance had boosted to thirty-two. Prayer meetings were set up once a week in different parishioners' homes. A Visiting Committee was organized, and people joined enthusiastically.

Gage was young and energetic. He had a nice two-story parsonage one block from the church, so he could walk to and from work. His salary was $25.00 per week. It was all new and exciting. His life was ahead of him and he was tackling it head on with vigor.

He sat in his office thinking of all that he had accomplished in a short time. He bowed his head and thanked God for this opportunity. He promised God, he would give his all each and every day for the Lord's work.

He sat back and looked at the picture above his desk. It was a picture of a sailor in a storm holding the wheel of a ship with both hands. Water was pouring in from the side. Behind the sailor was Jesus with one hand on the wheel and the other hand on the sailor's shoulder. The picture was his favorite.

The message was clear to him. "Go forward into the storm and be not afraid, for I am with you!"

This picture looked down on Gage every day. It was as if his motto for life hung in that picture.

There was a war raging in Europe and Asia. Could the United States remain neutral? This was the question on everyone's mind. But for now, the war seemed far away, and his work was here in Palmer, Massachusetts.

A meeting was organized with all the Protestant ministers from Palmer and two neighboring towns, Monson and Brimfield. It was decided they would meet once a month for fellowship and share concerns and ideas for church attendance.

Gage thought this was a good idea. Being a minister was not just a job, but a calling. Ministers worked alone in their churches. They were CEO's, therapists, marriage advisors, grief counselors and inspirational leaders. How about having to prepare at least one twenty minute sermon each week! It was demanding work, but Gage relished it. Having the chance to sit and talk with other ministers would be beneficial.

The Sunday after Christmas was a high point for the new minister, Reverend Hotaling. The pews were filled with 179 people. This topped Christmas Sunday, which saw only 123 people in attendance. His new programs seemed to be working. When he had started in September there were 97 members, and attendance for that first Sunday was 103 people.

He was filled with gratitude and took pride in the work he had done. He remembered the final words Jesus had spoken to his disciples in Matthew, "Therefore go and make disciples of all nations, baptizing them in the name of the Father, and of the Son, and of the Holy Spirit, and teaching them to obey everything I have commanded you. And surely I am with you always, even to the end of time."

FEBRUARY 21, 1945
IWO JIMA CEMETERY

THE MEN OF THE GRAVES REGISTRATION section
were led to the location where the cemetery would be
situated. It was on a plateau above the beach, near an
airfield.

They climbed up one terrace to get off the beach. Two steps forward, one step back. As soon as one pulled his foot out of the sand, any sign of his footprint disappeared as the fine sand/ash mix filled the vacated hole.

At the top of the terrace, the island opened up before them. It was a flat, barren landscape devoid of vegetation. The only color was gray and brown. There was smoke from burning vehicles at every point of the compass. Dust was blowing across the flat island with nothing to stop it. It rested in eyes, ears and in the mouth.

A large, conical shaped mountain dominated the landscape on the left. It went from one side of the island to the other. This was Mount Suribachi, supposedly an active volcano. The only thing spewing from the mountain now was Japanese artillery, reigning down havoc on the Marines on the island.

Gage thought of a lunar landscape. Yes, this is what the surface of the moon might look like. He thought of a song, "For the beauty of the earth." There wasn't much beauty here.

Dark. Desolate. Devoid.

This was his new home. For how long, he wondered. On the boat, everyone talked about securing the island in three days, five at the most.

A shell came in, and he dove into his newly dug foxhole. This was day three and the island was nowhere near secure. The fury of combat could be heard across the flat terrain. More shells were coming in, so he stayed in his foxhole.

Our Father who art in Heaven . . . It was not the first, nor would it be the last time he uttered this prayer.

How had he gotten to this place?

Orders were being yelled out. No time to ponder.

The men were ordered to scrounge the area for any supplies they could find. Everyone in his section was without gear, as it was in some boat out on the Pacific.

Gage continued to search for ponchos. This would provide some cover for the cold night ahead. He made sure everyone in the unit had at least one poncho.

Gage had celebrated his 29th birthday on January 21. He wasn't drafted. It wasn't mandatory he enter the service. He had a young wife and a newborn back in the States. He wondered about seeing thirty.

DECEMBER 8, 1941

I T WAS EARLY EVENING. Gage was in his study, collecting his thoughts. His father had kept a diary and taught his son about this family tradition.

Gage got his first diary for Christmas when he was ten. At the time, it was his most cherished gift. It seemed like he had been given the keys to manhood. His father wrote in his diary every evening, so Gage would honor him by doing likewise.

His thoughts were all over the map, unfocused and unbelieving. He needed to start writing to gather his emotions and to put some semblance of sanity to the sad circumstances. War had been declared.

Today has been one of the saddest days that I can remember. It will go down in history as the day when the United States declared war on Japan with only one member of Congress opposing it.

Yesterday was a peaceful Sunday, clear and bright, until the middle of the afternoon when the news came over the radio that the Japanese had attacked Pearl Harbor. It was almost unbelievable for a while, but the reports kept coming which confirmed it.

So today, most of us have gone around, doing our work as best we could, but with our spirits at a very, very low ebb. It doesn't seem possible yet. The day we have all dreaded, the day we never wanted to see come, and yet, the day which we felt was inevitable is here.

What the future will bring, no one knows. Some are already predicting that the war won't last six months, because we are so strong and ought to be able to wipe up the Japanese in no time. But I am afraid it will be a long drawn-out conflict, and that it will be many a day before we shall see peace again. And when we do, I'm sure our world will be quite different from what it is today.

At any rate, we, as ministers, have a real job; first, to maintain morale among our people; secondly, to maintain love towards our enemies; and thirdly, to begin planning how we can have a just and durable peace.

He sat for a moment, drained. He read the lines and was satisfied.

Go forward into the storm and be not afraid, for I am with you!

What a storm this would be. Gage got up from his chair, turned out the light to his study and went to bed.

FEBRUARY 21, 1945
NIGHT

THE SUN HAD GONE DOWN, and the temperature dropped. Gage lay down in his foxhole. He had on a flannel shirt, dungaree jacket and field jacket. Adorning his feet were two pairs of heavy socks and his combat boots. He wrapped the poncho around him like a blanket.

Sleep would not come easy. It kept getting colder as the night wore on. This was not like camping out as a Boy Scout.

So much death and destruction. The Japanese had not been obliterated from the island. They had survived seventy-four days of bombing and were fighting the Marines with a tenacious fury.

He prayed like he had never prayed before. He prayed for courage. He prayed for strength. He prayed for safety. He prayed that he would do his job; that he would face this storm with grace. He prayed for dignity under fire.

Mail had not been delivered in a while. He felt inside his field jacket pocket for the last letter he had received from his wife. She and their eleven month old son had to move back home with her parents in Albany, New York. The letter was still there and it gave him some comfort.

Letters. While he was working in the Palmer Church, he instituted a letter writing campaign for servicemen in the area. Most of the parishioners partook of this endeavor. Letters were sent so the boys fighting against tyranny would feel the backing from the folks on the home front.

As the war dragged on, Gage began to feel there was more for him to do. One year went by, then two. The calendar turned to 1944.

He could no longer stay on the sidelines. He was overtaken by an inner voice that gnawed at him. How would he be able to preach to this generation if he could not experience what they were going through? Men and women of his generation had gone off to war, and he had stayed safe on the home front. How could he help shape the peace, not having been a participant in bringing it about?

He prayed for guidance. Was this the path God wanted him to follow? The answer kept coming back, yes. He would leave the safety of his home, the love of his young bride and seeing his newborn son grow through those early formative years. It was not an easy decision, but he felt led in that direction. As a man of God, he could not turn his back on this calling.

He enlisted in the Navy in June 1944. Now, he was attempting to sleep in a cold foxhole, on an ugly island he had never heard of, in a combat zone. He was a Navy Chaplain assigned to the Marines. Chaplains and medical personnel with Marine units were all from the Navy. The Marines didn't have time to teach these disciplines. They taught everyone how to be . . .well, a Marine.

October, 1944
P.O.W. s

T HE CAMP WAS FILLED WITH GERMAN prisoners. In talking with them, Gage found they had been captured at Normandy. Many of them appeared too young for combat. Most of them had never taken a razor to their face. If this was all the Germans had left, perhaps the rumors would hold true. There was talk the Americans would be in Berlin before Christmas. Time would tell.

It was October, 1944, and Gage was spending an afternoon in a POW camp ninety-three miles from the Chaplain School in Williamsburg, Virginia. There were two others with him touring the camp. The Red Cross director was there to check on the condition of the camp and the health and well-being of the prisoners. According to the records, there were approximately 500 prisoners in this camp. They were being treated well and looked healthy. They were housed five to a hut. Was the enemy affording such care to American POW's? There was some doubt.

The young prisoners saluted Gage. How weird, he thought. He'd been in the Navy for only five weeks, and here he was being saluted by German prisoners on American soil. A most unusual experience.

It was cold, and he started to shiver. Why was it so cold in October? Where was he?

The cold woke him. What was he doing in this foxhole? Gage instinctively curled up and pulled the poncho around him to get warm. He had been asleep and dreaming of the POW camp he had visited four months earlier. It all seemed so real in his dream. He could see the camp clearly, but the cold jolted him back to reality.

He was in a foxhole on Iwo Jima. The vividness of the dream was a stark contrast to where he was. It was midnight by his watch.

The cold had penetrated deep into his bones. He shivered uncontrollably. He put his head into the poncho, breathing warm air towards his body curled up as tight as possible. The sound of sparse gunfire could be heard.

He thought of his lovely wife back home. Her blue eyes were burned into his memory. They were the prettiest things he could remember. *Goodnight, my sweet little Bright Eyes. Be sure to keep that smile there always for me. It's a thrill to know I've got the bestest little girl in the world waiting for me back home!* Their love had brought forth a son.

William Hotaling was born March 15, 1944. Seeing his newborn son behind the glass was a moment Gage would never forget.

Gage was an only child, never having to learn how to share affection with anyone other than his parents. Now, there was this helpless baby boy who would teach him how to love beyond himself. Gage felt his heart bursting with a different type of love never before experienced.

His son also meant the Hotaling name would be carried forward to the next generation. Gage lay shivering in his foxhole. The memories had not chased the cold away, but had made it more palatable. He asked God's special protection for them and soon fell back to sleep.

February 21, 1945

Terror

THE GROUND SHOOK, and the explosion woke him with a start. He heard the drone of airplanes, then more explosions nearby. He looked out from under his poncho to see Japanese planes flying over the island, dropping bombs on the Marines below.

First the dark, then the cold, now the bombs. *Dear Lord, what have you got me into?* He knew his heart worked, as it pounded in his chest.

A bomb exploded about 100 yards away. He could not tell if he shivered from cold or fear. His knuckles were clenched in fear, so much so, they began to cramp. He wanted to make himself smaller, but was curled up as tight as possible. He still felt too large. He felt the Japanese pilots could see him, and a bomb would find his foxhole.

Gethsemane. Jesus in the Garden sprung into his mind. Was this the type of fear his Lord suffered that night? Jesus knew he would die. Gage did not. Which was worse, he thought.

He heard the whistle of another bomb falling from the sky. The explosion was further away, yet jarring to his nerves. It was 0400 hours by his watch. Morning was too far away. He was living moment to moment in shear fear.

If you are standing by my shoulder Lord, it sure would be nice to feel you calm these nerves!

More whistles in the sky. More bombs were falling. Explosions were all around him.

He heard a Marine scream out at the planes, "I'll get you, you sons of bitches!"

Then there was rifle fire. This had little effect on the planes overhead. They were incessant as a swarm of bees. Gage prayed he would not be among their victims.

The noise of airplane motors receded. They were pulling away.

"Corpsman!" Came a yell from the dark. Someone had gotten hit and was in need of aid.

Names were being called out as men checked to see if their buddies were okay. Voices were answering "Okay" and "Yeah, I'm good."

"Hotaling!" His mind didn't register his name first.

"HOTALING, you okay?" The voice was louder.

"I'm okay," he responded. He was still shivering under his poncho, but he didn't seem to be hit.

Thank you, God. Gage offered this quick prayer.

"Decker, you okay?" was spoken in a sharp tone. There was no answer in the dark.

"Decker!"

Still no answer.

"Someone check on Decker"

The sound of airplanes returning filled the night sky. The Japanese had circled around and were making another bombing run over the island.

"Here they come again, boys!"

The whistles came first, then the explosions. Gage shrunk back under his poncho. More terror from the sky. Morning would allow for return fire, but it was still dark.

He was beginning to tell from the whistling bombs if they would hit close or further away.

His mind thought back to the chaplain he met in Hawaii. What was his name? Gage couldn't pull his name out from his brain while shivering. This chaplain had been in three operations with the Marines.

Samuels. That was his name.

Anyhow, Gage remembered Samuels speaking of being close to a nervous breakdown. Samuels would not put his wife's picture out, as looking at it got him terribly depressed. Gage hoped he would never get to a place where he wouldn't want Dell's picture in front of him.

The Division Chaplain, Harry Wood, confided in Gage that he hoped Samuels wouldn't go over the edge before he got relieved.

A whistle was heard falling close by. The explosion came, and he heard a scream. Then silence. There was no yell for a corpsman. Gage said a quick prayer for the man's soul.

Would morning ever get here? He made himself as small as he could get and waited. He thought again of Samuels, who had been in three operations. Gage had been on shore less than twenty-four hours in his first operation.

Lord, keep me from going off the deep end.

He hoped he could withstand the strain tearing at every pore. He hoped he would keep his wits.

Go forward into the storm and be not afraid, for I am with you.

FEBRUARY 22, 1945
MORNING

SLEEP HAD BEEN restless. Gage wasn't sure he even slept, for it seemed he had spent the latter part of the night in that stage between sleep and wakefulness.

"Hotaling, you in there?"

"Yeah, I'm okay."

He pulled the poncho back and saw it was daylight. It was also raining. He saw men standing around a fire.

The fire was inviting, so he crawled out from his foxhole, put the poncho around him to ward off the rain and joined the others. It felt good to be near some warmth.

"Anyone find Decker?"

"Yeah, he got hit with shrapnel pretty bad in the leg. It doesn't look good. He could lose it. He was taken to the beach earlier and transported to the hospital ship."

"Damn!"

Someone else said with a heavy dose of sarcasm, "Well, it's D plus 3, the island should be secure tonight."

"Right, that's what the brass said!"

There was muted laughter.

"Shit, you should know better than to believe all that pre-battle hype. That's just so the new guys won't get all worried. There's a lot of island to cover!"

Gage noticed sergeant stripes on this Marine. He had seen action before. This was a man to listen to.

The sergeant continued. "Last night was nothing. On every other island we've been on, the little yellow bastards have hit us with an all-out banzai attack, either the first or second night. Now that's some terror. You fight all day to get a secure beachhead and then when night comes, they attack, yelling and screaming. Your nerves are frayed, you're tired beyond description. You're reduced to primal instincts just to survive. That has not happened on this island, yet. I'll take a night of bombing over those damn banzai attacks."

The veterans agreed. There was a hush among the raw recruits, who were happy to have survived the night. If there was something more terrifying than last night, Gage did not wish to encounter it.

Everyone seemed lost in their thoughts as the rain came down in a steady, harsh manner.

The aroma was a strange mix. There was smoke, there was moisture and there was the ever present smell of sulfur. It had been reported the Japanese had mined this island for sulfur. It was plentiful.

The boys began spewing forth with their battle banter. It was about everything. It was about nothing. Whatever was said was usually disputed. It had no meaning. It was banter that helped pass the time. It was nervous energy just pouring out of mouths.

Gage's mind recalled a moment crossing the Pacific. He had been asked to preach one particular Sunday on the ship. There were several chaplains on board, so Sunday sermons were rotated. After the service, he received many compliments from the men who attended.

One boy spoke to him saying there was a small group that had started to meet each night for hymns and prayers. They met at 2000 hours, and this young Marine asked Gage if he would care to join them. He told the Marine he would be delighted to join them.

When he arrived that night, there were 20 Marines, and they sang every song from memory. It was a scene that seemed surreal. Here were twenty Marines heading into battle, on the deck of a warship, singing "Jesus Wants Me for a Sunbeam."

They sang songs and recited prayers for an hour. This was really inspiring fellowship with Gage. For the rest of the journey, he met on deck every night at eight for an informal get-together.

He didn't have to prepare anything for these services, which made them more meaningful and enjoyable. He was reminded of the early followers of Jesus, meeting in various places without the strict rigors of pomp and circumstance. How very refreshing. Gage enjoyed these meetings immensely.

FEBRUARY 22, 1945

NIGHT

T HE DAY HAD BEEN WET and uneventful. The rain, like the sound of combat, was a steady companion; dampening the skin, damaging the soul.

Gage was hardening to the mortar shells exploding nearby. He did not cringe at every noise as when he first hit the beach. Adaptation had settled in, and being in combat was his new normal. If a shell landed too close, he could sense it by a quick jitter inside. Otherwise, the explosions were mere background noise, as when a window was open on a warm spring day and all the outside noise would fill the room. Steady, yet unthreatening.

The day had been spent securing more gear. Blankets, shelter halves, mess kits and more ponchos. Each man in his unit would have more creature comforts than the previous night. Gage was in his foxhole with a blanket and poncho under him and an extra blanket on top. He was warm and hoped he could keep the cold at bay through the night.

The enemy was another story. Would they send planes again? He hoped not. His imagination ran wild with the thought of a banzai attack. Night can always make things more dreadful, and his mind took this fear to a new level.

The Marine sergeant had gone into detail about nocturnal banzai attacks. Gage was too busy during the day to dwell on such an event, but as he lay in his foxhole, it seemed to be all he could think about. He tried praying to calm his nerves. It worked as a temporary respite, but not long after his amen was a distant memory, his worst fears would again be his companion.

His thoughts drifted back to the uncomfortable nights below deck on board ship crossing the Pacific. His quarters were below deck in a room with other chaplains. There were no windows or portholes, only a door leading out. When night came, the doors were shut tight and lights were extinguished, as they were nearing enemy territory. The rooms were hot and stuffy, making sleep a most miserable experience.

Now, attempting to sleep in his foxhole, those stuffy nights on the ship became a pleasant memory. He prayed for at least one more boat ride across the Pacific in a conscious state.

FEBRUARY 23, 1945

EVENING

GAGE SAT IN HIS FOXHOLE reflecting on all that had happened. The previous night had brought no terror. He had slept comfortably through the night and when he awoke, it was morning and the sun was shining. The temperature rose with the sun. His clothes dried out and it seemed the sound of combat was further away.

The day was memorable to all, as the American flag was seen flying on top of Mount Suribachi. The Marines had scaled the mountain, mounted a large flag on a pole and hoisted it tall for all to see. All the ships in the harbor blew their horns. The boys in his section pointed excitedly to the flag. Field glasses were raised to get a closer view. They were all thrilled at the sight. Everyone was talking about the flag at chow.

"That flag standing tall and proud, lifted my spirits," said one Marine.

"Damn right!"

"*Semper fi*, baby, *semper fi*!"

Gage listened to all the boys as he ate. He was certainly a proud American this day.

"This island is considered Japanese territory. It is the first time we've planted the Stars and Stripes right down their yellow bellied throats! All the other islands we've taken were to expel the Japanese invader from land they conquered."

"That's right, Gleason. Now we're closing in on their homeland and we've set our boots and our flag on their soil. We'll show those sons of bitches!"

"Pearl Harbor. They asked for this and more! Here come the Marines."

"To the shores of Tripoli or Tokyo!"

This brought much laughter. The boys were in fine spirits.

Gage enjoyed all the banter. The boys were crude, they were loud, but damn, their words expressed how he felt inside. This would be a day he would remember for the rest of his life. He thanked the Lord for putting him in this place.

He opened the last letter from his wife. He had it memorized, but the words filled his heart with joy. He savored every word, reading it slowly, as if for the first time.

1930s

LEARNING THE CRAFT

___

G

AGE STUDIED MANY DIFFERENT preachers while in seminary. He was looking for the voice he would like to portray in his pulpit. He was also looking for ministers he would most like to emulate in his professional life. He journeyed to many churches and religious meetings.

Being a preacher's kid, his dad had been an early influence on him. But the person who first introduced Gage to the possibility of what preaching could be was Charlie Taylor, one of the great evangelists of his day. Gage first heard Charlie preach on February 5, 1933. Gage was thrilled with Taylor's personality, his smile and his voice. That voice preached one heck of a sermon that kept Gage's interest from beginning to end. His eyes were opened to the great possibilities that preaching could be. Something was stirred inside the soul of the aspiring young preacher.

Gage would listen to Charlie Taylor many times over the next three weeks. When Taylor moved on, Gage sat down and wrote his thoughts in his diary. The following excerpt is from February 27, 1933:

Charlie has been here for three weeks and is gone. I have heard him twenty-two times and feel that it isn't half enough. Always he is through with his sermon before I am ready to go—I could listen a half hour longer. Charlie Taylor intrigues and fascinates me. He makes me wish I could preach like that. What a thrill it must be to hold an audience spellbound with the ridiculously easy flow of words which he has. Truly a master if I ever saw one!

The net result has been this—my interest in sermons and preaching has been aroused! I inevitably compare Dad's sermons with Charlie's now and wish Dad could put as many illustrations in his preaching as Charlie does. Charlie's sermons must be typical of the new age. I haven't been interested before. Now I shall examine each and every sermon I hear.

His sojourn was at its beginning. Here was preaching with relevance in it. Here was preaching that was alive. Here was preaching he would aspire to. Here was the craft he would create for himself.

On an April Sunday in 1934, he attended a local Church service. The preaching was quite a disappointment to Gage. He went for a long walk after the service to ponder. He was deeply disgusted with what he had heard. There was no life in the sermon. It occurred to him if he couldn't do any better than what he'd just heard, he'd hang himself.

He said to his Lord on that walk: "I don't think I'll ever hear worse preaching. Let this be a lesson to me. Preaching Preaching must have life in it and must carry a convincing message!" "

He had discovered how not to preach, and this lifeless sermon would always be in the back of his mind to remind him. Gage wondered how this preacher ever expected to win anyone to Christ?

There were others who inspired him as well. Dr. William Stidger was a preacher of "symphonic" sermons.

Instead of three or four main points, he had one fundamental idea which ran throughout his sermons. This idea was contained in one sentence which was catchy and easy to remember. This type of preaching appealed to Gage , and he began to hone his "symphonic" preaching skills.

One Sunday, the Rev. Carl H. Kopf, of the Mt. Vernon Congregational Church in Boston, came to do a Vesper Service at Andover Newton, the seminary Gage attended. Many of his classmates had been raving about this man's preaching.

Gage was mesmerized. The man had pulpit presence, power in delivery and words that struck deep. He began with a strong opening sentence and kept the pace up all the way through. He seemed to be a master of public speaking. This man was as close to an ideal preacher as anyone he'd ever heard!

After the service, Rev. Kopf sat with the seminarians in an informal gathering, teaching and answering all their questions. Gage took copious notes.

Rev. Kopf told the students when he was young, he attempted to preach like Dr. Harry Emerson Fosdick, but discovered it didn't work. His advice to young preachers was, "Tell no story but your own"! He went on to say, "One of the saddest things in life would be to be Dr. Fosdick and not be able to quote Dr. Fosdick."

Gage was fascinated and writing as fast as he could.

Then Rev. Kopf uttered these words, "Most preachers begin at a point which the audience has not yet reached and continue by a process of logic to a point which the audience never will reach. They are thus engaged in nothing more than sacred solitaire."

He went on to say, "You must preach to the things around you. Why use a text that is 2000 years old? When Jesus preached, he used things from everyday life, 'A sower went forth to sow.'"

Gage was stunned by the force and simplicity of these teachings. This man not only knew how to preach, but he was an excellent educator.

Gage saw that Rev. Kopf lived for his preaching. This was truly a passion to aspire to. Gage would add this to his mantra; I am to live for my preaching! He asked God to keep him ever true to that.

Dr. Norman Vincent Peale always spoke with a positive outlook on life. He did not dwell on sin and how bad mankind was. This also appealed to Gage.

He had heard them all preach and he took something from each to add to the voice he was creating.

One book that he kept close was entitled *Preach It Again*, by Dr. Clausen. He would make frequent use of this book. In it were these qualities of a good sermon:

A sermon must be interesting;
A sermon must be brief;
A sermon must use the news;
A sermon must be simple;
A sermon must be dramatic;
Make every sermon an event!

These phrases would become his sermon mantra. He would be a craftsman doing the Lord's work. He was conscious that God would be utilizing his talents in some large place of service. This gave him the ambition to always continue to improve.

February 23, 1945
Darkness Comes Again

GAGE HAD JUST FINISHED READING the last letter from Dell. He more quoted it from memory than actually read it. He wished her goodnight across the miles and did the same for his son.

Lord, keep them safe in your care. This he prayed as he lay in his foxhole.

It was dark, and his mind wondered what tonight might bring. He had encountered one night of enemy bombing and one night of sleep. Would there be more planes? Would there be the dreaded banzai attack? Would there be nothing?

Yea, though I walk through the valley of the shadow of death, I will fear no evil for thou art with me.

He prayed quite a few more lines before slowly drifting off to sleep.

The sounds woke him up. There was the drone of airplanes, the whistles of bombs falling and the explosions. He looked at his watch. It was 9:45. This would be a long night.

He heard a different sound. Ack-ack-ack.

"The Navy's giving 'em hell!"

He looked out and saw an incredible sight. The sky was lit up like the Fourth of July. The Navy was firing tracer anti-aircraft bullets at the Japanese planes. There was a steady stream of light shooting from the ships into the sky. Hundreds of lines of lights looking like V's as they rose from each deck. Each V had its own distinct origin. Each V was filled with numerous lines of light.

He also saw groups of light falling slowly to the ground. They had a magical quality. He thought of a Great Blue Heron standing still on a pond, stalking in its stillness for a meal. The top of the light was the heron's head. A thick light fell away from the head toward the ground. This was the body. There were three to four thinner strands of light falling away looking like legs.

Gage chuckled to himself. It reminded him of a game Dell had taught him. They would lie in the grass and look at clouds. Then they would say what shapes they saw in the various clouds. They would laugh at each other and have a delightful time. Here he was in combat doing the same with weapons of destruction. What looked like a heron were illuminating shells fired by the Navy into the sky. They would reach a certain height, illuminate and then slowly descend to the ground lazily under a parachute. The sky was as pretty a sight as he could ever remember seeing.

Bombs were exploding. Planes were buzzing. Ships were expelling antiaircraft fire into the air. The cacophony of combat was all around him. Yet he was filled with a boyish wonder, seeing the beauty of it all. This was better than anything he had seen on the big silver screen back home. Hollywood could not compare to this.

Gage did not shiver in fear. He was growing more accustomed to the constant companion of combat.

As suddenly as it started, it came to an end. The Navy had done its job and the Japanese planes had left. Some forever, some to fight another day.

He lay in his foxhole watching the show in the sky. The tracer bullets were no longer evident, but the Navy continued firing illuminating shells into the sky at steady intervals. Night had become day.

He watched as each shell burst into light and then slowly took the shape of the heron. It was quite the sight. The lights had a hypnotic effect, and soon he fell asleep.

Gage was awoken by the sounds of shells passing overhead.

Now what?

A quick glance at his watch told him it was 2425 hours. He was not going to enjoy sleep this night. He didn't hear planes. That was good news.

He glanced out of his foxhole to see what he could make of the shelling. There was fire coming from inland and it was passing overhead landing down near the beach. This was ground artillery.

The Japanese were firing at our guns along the beach. The Marines quickly responded, sending their own artillery shells back toward the enemy.

He watched and listened. The shells were passing overhead, going one way, then the other. He felt safe for the present, but he would not be able to get back to sleep, as the duel continued incessantly through the night.

January, 1945

Fellowship on the Deck

G AGE ENJOYED MEETING with the Marines on deck every night. It was cooler than being shut up below deck in his berth.

He noticed most of the boys were from the South. He had always heard the Southerners were much better at attending church than people from the North. He wasn't sure why this was, but it certainly held true with this small group.

They were not afraid to talk about their religion openly and deeply. They were not as reserved as the people from New England he was used to. This was quite refreshing.

Gage taught them some of the songs he had learned at various Baptist camps he had attended. Soon, everyone was singing these new songs as if they had grown up with them.

One night, Gage suggested they meet during the day so they could get better acquainted. This idea was met with much agreement. They decided to meet at 1300 hours on deck.

Now, he had two informal fellowship meetings to attend each day. It would help with the boredom of staring at the endless miles of ocean.

On February 6, 1945, they had their first daylight meeting on deck. Everyone shook hands and exchanged pleasantries. It was good to put a face to a voice. The afternoons became a time for informal chats. The evenings were their prayer and song time.

After one afternoon chat, a young Marine approached Gage to say that the boys were discussing his sermon the past Sunday after church. The Marine went on to say this was the first time he could remember the boys discussing a sermon since he had been in the Marines.

Gage thanked him, trying not to show how elated he felt inside. It showed he had given the boys something to think about. Maybe he had some service to perform out here on the ocean.

Each day, more and more Marines were joining their group. One day, a Marine from Swampscott, Massachusetts, joined in. Then on another day, one joined from Maine. These were the only two who came from New England.

Marines from different parts of the country were slowly drifting into this fellowship group, but Gage noticed a majority of the boys were from the South or California. The informal chats were invigorating as opinions varied from the different states.

One thing they all agreed on was the sooner the war was over, the better. They were all anxious to get back home, but until then, they were willing to push the Japanese Army all the way to Tokyo, if need be.

Gage enjoyed the chats and nightly fellowship. The men ran the show, and he was not responsible for having to prepare anything. What a way to travel across the Pacific!

FEBRUARY 24, 1945

I N THE MORNING, the Graves Registration section moved to different foxholes.

The enemy had been pushed back, and front line personnel support troops were moved closer to the fighting. They left many well-built foxholes behind. Gage settled into his new foxhole. Compared to where he had slept for three nights, his new home was elegant. It was lined with ninety-six sandbags on all four sides.

His new foxhole buddy was a young second lieutenant from Buffalo, New York, named Jack Greeno. Together, they rigged up good shelter over the top, consisting of a poncho and two shelter halves. This would help them stay dry.

Lt. Greeno was the division personal effects officer, who was responsible for sending the personal effects of dead Marines home to the families.

"Chaplain, eh. Is this your first time in combat?"

"Does it show?" Gage wondered how he could tell.

"I thought so. You've just got that look. It can get pretty rough and gruesome. I hope you're tough enough. This ain't like Navy shore duty in Hawaii."

This fired up some adrenaline inside Gage. He would show this young lieutenant what he was made of. *If the likes of you can handle this, then I am sure I can too!* "We'll see what I can do" was all he said to Greeno.

Their eyes met. Gage nodded his head in recognition of the challenge and his willingness to be tested. Greeno nodded back.

With the Graves Registration section, one of Gage's duties involved collecting personal effects from the bodies of dead Marines. He knew this task would test him as nothing he had experienced before.

Yesterday, he had been given another order. He was to count the dead bodies every day at 1600. The bulldozers had been working hard to prepare the cemetery to receive its first inhabitants. There was talk the first burials could be today.

As he began his first count, he was filled with a strange sense of dread. He looked at the row of bodies covered with ponchos. All the hopes, dreams and aspirations of these young men had been extinguished. Back home would be grieving mothers, fathers, siblings, girlfriends, wives, and in some cases, children. His heart was heavy.

My God, forgive us all for what we do to each other.

He knew war had filled the history of mankind. The *Old Testament* was filled with accounts of warfare between the Hebrew people and their neighbors. But all that he read could not prepare him for this moment of seeing the destruction of so many young lives by combat.

It was now up close and personal. He wondered if God wept. He knew Jesus did. He was reminded of the shortest verse in the Bible found in *John 11:35*: "Jesus wept."

His nose was overtaken by a new odor. The stench of death, his brain told him. It was foul. It was repugnant. It was unnerving. He was breathing fast. His heart was pounding as though it would explode out of his chest. He felt lightheaded and unsteady.

Go forward into the storm and be not afraid . . .

His brain could not finish the thought. He felt no hand on his shoulder. He felt alone. Still, he had a job to do.

He began to count the bodies from a distance that enabled him to perform his task without getting too close. The odor still bothered him. He reached into his pocket and found the cigarettes from his C-rations. He had never smoked in his life, but he had been around people who smoked, and felt the smell would be better than the odor emanating from the corpses.

He put a cigarette between his lips, lit it, took a drag and coughed fiercely. *Just puff it and hold it in your mouth for a moment.* He took a small drag and held it in his mouth before blowing it out. This worked better for him. He stood on a small island in the middle of the Pacific Ocean, smoking his first cigarette, thinking of yet another new experience in life he could attribute to the war.

Lord, forgive me this small transgression as I deal with man's inhumanity to man.

He saw some people spraying the corpses with what looked like water from a hose. He watched them work from body to body, spraying each one while he smoked. Soon, he knew it wasn't water, as the scent of chemicals filled the air. When they were finished Gage walked over to inquire what they were doing.

"We spray the corpses with disinfectant. It helps prevent the spread of disease. These are lessons we learned from other islands."

APRIL 11, 1943

AGE WAS IN HIS STUDY. It was Sunday night and the day had been a trying one for him.
He began to write in his diary.

This has been a sad, strange day. The first news that greeted me this morning was that both Mrs. Squires and Jimmy Payne died during the night. Both have been among the most faithful supporters of the church, and both have been sick with cancer for months.

I had to announce their deaths at the morning service, and there was a profound sense of shock when I did so. The sermon I had written for today, "Are You Tired of Being Brave?" could not have been more appropriate. It seemed to just fit the occasion. It certainly was not easy to get through the day, but by the grace of God I was able to do so. I doubt I'll ever have anything just like this again, where two prominent members of the church both die the same night, and the news is the first thing to reach me Sunday morning.

Gage stopped writing and read the lines he had written. Nothing needed to be added, so he put the pen down and closed the diary.

He looked at the picture over his desk. He felt the presence of a hand on his shoulder and it gave him a sense of comfort.

He had weathered this storm.

FEBRUARY 24, 1945

HE NEW ORDERS TERRIFIED HIM.

He would now be probing amongst the dead Marines, clearing their pockets of all personal items so they could be sent home to grieving family members.

Sending the effects home was the job of his new foxhole mate, Lt. Greeno. Now, Gage had to retrieve these effects so Lt. Greeno could perform his clean task. Who had the more gruesome job now?

Gage took a pile of bags with him and walked over to the row of bodies he was ordered to search. He lit a cigarette as he approached his appointed duty. He made sure he had plenty of cigarettes, even trading for some from other members of his unit who didn't smoke. Since his first encounter, counting the dead yesterday, the aroma of smoke was an ever-present scent filling both his nose and mouth.

He reached the first dead Marine, who looked too young to be in combat. His face was smooth and appeared to have never been touched by a razor. Gage said a quiet prayer for the young man's soul to be accepted into his Father's heavenly home. One dog tag was cut off and placed in a bag. Gage found a wallet with a small amount of money, which he inventoried. There were pictures of his parents and some with other young people. They could have been siblings, friends or a combination of both. The wallet with the money was dropped into the bag along with the inventoried list. Gage spent another moment over the boy with a heavy heart.

Sleep well with the angels.

The cigarette was at its end. Gage flicked it into the sand and reached for another. He lit it and moved to the next body.

One leg was badly mangled and there were flies and maggots infesting the leg. His mind was repulsed and his heart raced. He puffed heavily on the cigarette and held the smoke in his mouth, until his whole brain seemed filled with the aroma of tobacco. Then he exhaled slowly, trying to calm his nerves.

He repeated this process one more time until it seemed he had a grip on himself. A dog tag was placed into the bag, as was a watch. The wallet showed a picture of a young woman holding a baby.

Gage pulled the picture out and read the back. On it was written, "Your beautiful bride and baby girl. Come home to us."

His heart sank. His eyes filled with tears. A family was torn apart. This young baby girl would never know her father.

Gage felt tears trickle down his face. He looked at all of the bodies he was assigned to inventory and he was overcome with a tremendous sense of sadness.

December 11, 1943

Tragedy

I T WAS A HARD FUNERAL to perform, but it was part of a minister's job. One of his parishioners with a wife and two young children was killed in a tragic accident while at work.

The week had been filled with tending to the grieving family. When Gage heard the news, he went to the house to offer whatever he could to the family. He wasn't sure what he would say or what comfort he could offer.

As a minister, this was the first tragedy he would face. One of his flock was now in deep distress over a death. A death that would rob this family of a husband and a father.

When Gage got to the house, the children were still at school and the widow was quite dazed. She cried on his shoulder, spilling out some of her grief. Gage let her cry and just held her. It was not an angry or hysterical cry, but a soft cry of realization. Realization that her husband was gone and would not ever come home. Realization that her children would never see their father again. Her sobs were subdued.

Gage offered some words, but even he was not sure if they were the right things to say in this situation.

She asked him to call her family in the neighboring town and tell them the news. She didn't feel up to it. Gage called her parents and broke the news to them. He hung up the phone and informed her they would come over as quickly as they could to be with her. She nodded through moist eyes.

Gage was impressed with her demeanor. Yes, she was dazed, but she did not go into hysterics or become irrational at any time. He continued sitting with her and let her talk. He felt he could be of service by staying with her and remaining calm.

He asked her if he could say a prayer for her husband's soul and to pray for her comfort. She agreed, so they spent a few moments in prayer. When her parents arrived, he offered his condolences, got up to leave and informed them he would stay in touch.

As he left, feelings of inadequacy came over him. Had he been of any help? Had he said the right words to offer comfort? He wasn't sure.

Lord, I ask for your forgiveness if I've failed you today. Whatever my shortcomings, send your angels of comfort to this family and surround them with your love and mercy.

The funeral on December 11th, was a solemn affair, with many family members sitting in the front rows. Co-workers and friends filled the church to capacity. There was music, there were words spoken by family members, and Gage did his part as the minister.

When the service was over, Gage stood at the back of the church shaking hands, thanking people for attending, and offering more words of comfort to family members.

The man's widow gave him a hug, then stepped back. She held his arms and told him what a great comfort he had been that first afternoon. He was stunned by her remark. He felt he had not done enough.

That night in his study, he thought of her words and the past three days. He opened his diary and wrote these words:

The funeral was a tremendous emotional experience because it seemed almost as though I became a member of the family and shared the sorrow with them. I suppose there is no greater feeling of kinship a pastor can ever have with any of his parishioners than to travel the road of sorrow and tragedy with them as I have done the last three days.

The words had captured his feelings. They had come from deep inside. Or were they from a greater power? He wasn't sure, but he was satisfied with their message.

His journey as a minister was maturing.

February 24, 1945

Chaplains on Iwo Jima

Gage Hotaling 2nd from left

THE DAY WORE ON. One body after another, one cigarette after another—a metronome of misery.

Gage had locked his emotions somewhere deep inside so he could continue to do his job.

He wondered if Lt. Greeno was tough enough for this job. A question he would gladly ask the young lieutenant later.

After this ordeal, counting the bodies at 1600 would be a snap.

Gage came upon his next dead Marine. He cut off one dog tag and then reached into the pockets for belongings. His hand grabbed something moist causing him to remove it quickly. Turning the hand over Gage was confronted by body parts. He wasn't sure what it was, but he knew immediately it was from the dead Marine.

There was a small retch from his stomach. He refused to lose it. By sheer will, he stopped the bile in his throat and swallowed hard. Quickly he plunged his hand into the sand, moving it around until all the ooze was gone.

His emotions escaped from their inner prison and welled up inside of him. Revulsion was at the forefront. He sat down in the sand to gather himself. Then he lit another cigarette. Slowly he inhaled, and ever so slowly, he exhaled, as if to expel all the revulsion he was feeling. He would have to steel his nerves to this type of moment, both now and for the future.

He pulled out the small book of *Psalms* he carried in his pocket and opened it. It fell open at *Psalm 102*. Gage read the first three verses.

"Hear my prayer, O Lord, and let my cry come unto thee. Hide not thy face from me in the day when I am in trouble; incline thine ear unto me: in the day when I call answer me speedily."

He sat on the volcanic sand, reflecting on these words, while smoking. The day had brought much trouble, yet he felt a steely resolve come over him, a resolve that seemed to be saying this ordeal would be weathered. He felt that invisible hand on his shoulder and a calmness settling in.

Orders were given that the first burials would commence after midday chow.

Gage had watched as the engineers went over the cemetery area with mine detectors. As soon as it was deemed clear, the bulldozers scooped out a large trench. The cemetery was now ready.

The first row contained fifty bodies. When the whole row was covered over, Gage went with two boys from the unit who placed a flag on each individual grave.

Gage walked to the end of the first grave and uttered these words: "You have gallantly given your life on foreign soil in order that others might live. Now we commit your body to the ground, in the name of the Father, the Son and the Holy Ghost. May your soul rest in eternal peace. Amen."

He then repeated these words for each of the fifty graves.

June 7, 1939
Graduation from Seminary

THIS WAS THE FIRST STEP in Gage's journey to continue the work of his father. Ira would only be there in spirit, but it was a spirit that would be ever-present.

There was a black and white photograph which Gage had framed and placed at the top of his desk. It was taken in the backyard of their Providence, Rhode Island, home.

Ira sat in a chair, dressed in a light-colored suit with a white shirt and dark tie. Gage sat on the arm of the chair with a dark jacket, light pants, a dark tie and feet adorned with saddle shoes, the style of the day. This photograph would always be present as a constant reminder of Gage's calling.

Gage was looking forward to this day for two reasons. The first being the beginning of his life's professional journey. The second was to hear the speaker at the commencement, Dr. Arbuckle, one of Gage's favorite professors at Andover Newton. This man taught more than preaching. In his classes he gave his views on theology, the ministry as a profession and church work.

Gage recalled the classes as rare treats. Dr. Arbuckle would begin the lecture with Biblical material and then would talk about something from his own experiences.

Gage considered him a realist and a modernist. He considered the man's views not founded upon any creed, but upon thirty years of growing and thinking. This was a man Gage would hope to emulate.

The commencement speech was memorable for Gage. One quote that would stick with him was this: "For the last three years we have been appraising you; for the next thirty years you will be appraising us."

Gage felt the power of this statement as it was uttered. This man knew how to put words together to address an audience, to keep their interest and to leave them with thought provoking material.

There was even some humor thrown into the speech. Dr. Arbuckle spoke of the worry that students faced over passing exams. He called this useless worry, because the faculty are under the necessity of passing the students so that the alumni body will be continued. "This thing has to go on!"

This line received the most laughter from the audience, especially the students, who had spent the past three weeks worrying about just this.

With his diploma in his hand, Gage went into the audience to share this moment with the two most important people in his life. They were his mother Albertha and his fiancé Dell Bauer. He was jubilant with his diploma and sharing it with these two women. One who represented his youth and upbringing and one who represented his future. This was a day of endings, but also a day for new chapters to begin in his life.

MARCH, 1945

THERE ARE NO WORDS

NECESSARY

February 25, 1945 – 100 men buried.
February 26, 1945 – 105 men buried.
February 27, 1945 – 95 men buried.
February 28, 1945 – 200 men buried.

GAGE WAS EATING CHOW with members of his unit. Everyone was eating silently, lost in their own thoughts. Burying row upon row of dead Marines was not an easy task. It took its toll. The numerous burials seemed to be piling on his soul, slowly tightening, bringing more and more heaviness to his hardened insides. He could feel no hand on his shoulder. He seemed adrift in a sea of death.

A Marine correspondent sat down and asked about everyone's duties. No one knew how to respond, except with unbelieving stares.

"We bury the dead!" a voice said icily.

Gage asked the correspondent to go outside for a walk with him. When they were away from the others, Gage tried to explain the cold reception. Theirs was a grim job. No one wished to glorify it or speak of it. Gage told him of collecting personal effects, counting bodies and of course of the committal services.

He paused for a moment and then said, "Most jobs you can get used to. But this one is different. Every man you bury is a fresh tragedy."

The correspondent thanked Gage for his time, nodded and walked off.

February 28, 1945
Casualties Hit Home

THE SOUND OF COMBAT was off in the distance. The Marines had pushed their lines further up the island toward the northeast. During the past four days as burials were taking place, mortar shells were still being fired by the Japs. Most of them did not come close to disturbing any burials, and except for the constant background noise, they were not too disconcerting to the men of the Graves Registration section.

There had been no casualties and very few close calls in the preceding four days. The men of the section felt safer as each day passed.

That sense of safety was shattered this day. Mortar shells and sniper fire were zeroed in on the men as they worked. A mortar shell landed by a bulldozer in the cemetery, which was within fifty feet of where the men were working.

Burials were halted and each man scrambled for a foxhole.

Gage got to his foxhole and peered over the top. Sniper fire was hot and heavy. The Marines were responding with fire of their own, shooting back at flashes that appeared from enemy guns.

"I'm hit in the leg and need help getting to cover!"

"Covering fire!"

The Marines opened up with a fury. Gage watched as a Marine ran to the wounded man, put him over his shoulder, and carried him back to a foxhole. They both got back unscathed.

"Medic!"

Sniper fire was still coming in, so Gage sank down beneath the sandbags. He did not wish to end up at the wrong end of a sniper's bullet.

This was the first day enemy fire had interfered with his work. He felt a sense of fear similar to what he had experienced that first night on Iwo. He said a quick prayer to help calm the nerves.

It got quiet. The shelling had stopped. Gage peered over the top. Men were looking around and some were climbing out of their foxholes.

The sniper fire was no more. The Marines had eradicated the enemy snipers, or they had vanished into the belly of the island to fight another day.

The fighting on this island was different than anything the Marines had experienced before. The Japanese did not fight from behind surface barriers, or out in the open. They seemed to come up from within the island, shoot, and then disappear back into the island. The Marines talked openly of the Japanese having a massive underground cave system.

Activity commenced at the cemetery. Bodies were being carried to their final resting spot, the big trench, for burial.

Gage climbed out of his foxhole to get back to work. He watched four men carrying a stretcher with a dead body, heading for the trench, when one of the men stepped on a land mine. The explosion knocked Gage to the ground and left his ears ringing.

He did a quick check of his body parts and found everything was still attached. Except for the ringing in his ears, he was fine.

Not so fortunate were the stretcher bearers. One man had his leg blown off and he was crying in pain. Two others had some shrapnel injuries.

Four casualties in the Graves Registration section, one serious, all in the span of an afternoon. There was no safe place in a combat zone.

February 15, 1945
A Letter Home

4th Marine Division

February 15, 1945
Dearest Darling Dell,

It's been three months since I was detached from Williamsburg. Five months ago today I was sworn into the Navy. And five years ago today I was ordained. How time flies when you look back in retrospect! Those precious days of '39 and '40 seem so near at times, as though they were just yesterday. And I can't make it seem possible that we lived in Palmer for four years.

Today I opened your extra long and extra enjoyable letter of Jan. 19th. You asked me why I suggested that you read the first two chapters of

Guadalcanal Diary. That's easy enough to guess. It's so you would have a picture of shipboard life and a landing on enemy soil.

Today is the hottest day yet. It's just like that torrid Sunday at Ocean Park when we invited George and Charlie for an ice cold drink after the evening service in the temple. Gee, how I wish I could go to the ice box right now and draw out an ice cold bottle of ginger ale or root beer, or Coca Cola! However, we can be thankful for one thing, and that is that we're not right on the equator.

I was happy when you told me how mother had put her arms around you and said, "Bless you, I love you, dear." I guess it takes something like me being so far away to make her feel different about things. Maybe she is even being affected like I am, so that just as I am learning to appreciate more the simple everyday elements of family life, she is too. It wouldn't surprise me the least.

There's no moon tonight, but I'll be outside for awhile on deck, and I'll be thinking of you, and wishing I could love you. How much you inspire me every day!

Darling, you're absolutely and unequivocally terrifically wonderful! A big hug for Billy, love for the folks, millions of kisses for you!

Always, your loving chaplain,

Gage

MARCH 1, 1945

G AGE FELT HIMSELF HARDENING inside. Retrieving personal effects from dead Marines, counting the dead and burying the dead were his daily tasks. He would not shirk his duty. He would not back down from his assigned jobs.

The Marines were fighting a stubborn enemy, an enemy that was holed up within the island. An enemy that was not acting predictably by launching banzai attacks at night that diminished their numbers. The Marines were caught in a fierce struggle for survival on this tiny island. Gage saw the results and knew if they were giving their all, he had to do likewise.

Death and destruction were all around him. He could see these two intertwined facets wherever he looked. Their smell filled his senses, together with the constant odor of tobacco. He knew he would never smoke again if he got off this island. Even if he enjoyed the aroma, which he didn't, the smell of tobacco, he feared, would always seem to remind him of this desolate place.

While moving among the dead on the beach, he heard his name being called.

"Hotaling, all our gear has just landed on the beach. Come on down and get your stuff."

Gage followed the boys down to the boat to retrieve his gear. He went on board and found his pack and his typewriter. There was no sign of his communion kit. He inquired, but was told by those driving the boat they were ordered to take these items to shore. They couldn't help him with anything else.

Gage left the boat with his pack and typewriter and walked to the cemetery. He wanted to get these to his foxhole.

"What you got, Chaplain?" inquired one of the boys in his section.

"Boys, all our gear is down at the beach aboard an LSM," said Gage.

"Only took eight days!" came a reply in a somewhat sarcastic tone.

"Let's get a truck and bring it all back. Be nice to have a change of clothes."

Yells of agreement met this statement.

The boys of the Graves Registration section requisitioned a truck, drove down to the beach, loaded all their gear and bought it back to their island home near the cemetery.

Gage found out his communion kit never left the transport. Now that transport was on its way with a load of casualties to either Saipan or Guam. He knew it would be a while before he saw that communion kit again, if ever.

There were more surprises in store this day. Mail was flown in for the first time since they were on the island. When the mail was distributed, Gage had six new letters from Dell. His evening would bring welcome words from home.

Most of his gear and six new letters! It was a banner day.

Before he sat down to read the letters he had one important entry to make in his daily log book:

March 1, 1945 – 100 men buried.

1941

CONTINUING EDUCATION

S CHOOLING HAD ALWAYS come easy for Gage. His grades were so good that he was pushed one year ahead of his classmates, graduating from high school at the age of 16. In Boy Scouts he attained the rank of Eagle. He didn't have siblings to fight with.

As a minister, he began to deal with people and their problems. This was something with which he had little firsthand experience.

He read a book entitled *Pastoral Psychiatry*, by Dr. John Sutherland Bonnell. He found it a most fascinating book on the subject of human problems. In the book, the author wrote about the many problems he had encountered as a minister and the various conversations and cures that were affected. It was a wonderful case study in behaviors a parish minister might encounter and how to deal with them.

As a young minister starting out, Gage took copious notes while reading the book. He began to keep his own book on human problems.

It occurred to him that a minister should be equally equipped in two great fields; preaching and pastoral work. He knew he had much to learn about dealing with human problems. This book would be his guide.

There was a course he did not have time to take while at Andover Newton. This course was on pastoral psychology and was called "Guiles' Personality Study." He looked through a current course catalog and found the course was being offered in the fall semester on Wednesday afternoons. He could drive to Newton from Palmer in an hour and a half and the travel would not bother him. He would have to clear it with his parish and make sure it would not interfere with his full-time duties. They were, after all, paying his salary.

Yes, he had an undergraduate degree from Brown University and a graduate degree from Andover Newton Theological School, but he knew there was still so much to learn. He could learn some by reading, but he felt he needed to take this course. Gage presented his reasons to the powers to be in the church. They listened and then gave him their blessing. He was off for more schooling.

MARCH 2, 1945

THERE SEEMED TO BE more bodies being prepared for burial today than Gage had encountered since being on the island. It would be a busy day. He could feel that hand on his shoulder and it gave him strength.

He remembered all the ribbing flung his way on the boat ride across the Pacific. He had expected some of it since it was his first operation, but the boys seemed to lay it on quite heavily. He wouldn't sleep. He wouldn't eat. He would lose weight and the smell of dead bodies would sicken him and make him puke. If that wasn't enough, the sight of maggots and flies crawling all over the bodies would surely finish him.

He had his moments when he began, but he had overcome them. He remembered almost losing his lunch the first day his hand was covered in bloody body parts. He was amazed at his own inner strength and fortitude. There was a deep well of toughness inside he had never drawn from before. He wondered if he would reach the bottom of that well before this battle ended.

His Division Chaplain, Harry Wood, had sent Chaplain Sneary to relieve Gage. He was to spend the day away from the cemetery and get a little rest and relaxation. This was his tenth straight day of duty since landing on Iwo.

Gage went back to his foxhole and read the letters he had received yesterday. They brought a smile to his face and helped relieve some his stress.

Then he tried reading a book, but his mind could not comprehend the words. He read sentence after sentence, but nothing stuck. It was a futile effort, so he put the book down.

He went to the company CP (command post) and spent time visiting and shooting the breeze. He was getting caught up on all the scuttlebutt. This had been the toughest island the Marines had encountered. It was taking far longer to conquer than anyone had imagined. And the casualties were enormous. This Gage knew of first hand. The flag had been flying on Suribachi for eight days, yet the island was nowhere near secure.

As good as it was to be away from duty for a while, he was getting a gnawing feeling in his gut to get back to work. Boys were fighting and dying. What right did he have to sit and chew the fat while staring out at the Pacific Ocean?

He tried to tell himself he deserved some down time, but it was an argument not to be won this day.

All right, Lord, I guess it's back to work.

He walked back to the cemetery. When he crested the first terrace and saw the island before him there was smoke and dust and the ever-present drone of combat. He could see the engineers blowing up one cave after another. This was necessary to keep the Japanese from using them again.

When he got to the cemetery, he reported to Chaplain Wood and informed him he did not need any more relief. He was ready to go back to work. Wood nodded his approval with a slight smile. There were plenty of burials to attend to.

That night after supper, Gage conducted a small worship service for the men of his outfit. They had been requesting this for several days, but this was the first opportunity that presented itself for such an occasion. It was a short service of scripture and prayer. The boys thanked Gage for his words. He sensed the service seemed to make them feel better.

He was tired from his long day. The burials had been numerous. He remembered the words the Catholic chaplain uttered at chow; "There must be something more to life than this. Otherwise, these boys have all had a rotten deal!"

Amen to that, he thought.

He tallied up the day's work. It astounded him when he saw the figure. No wonder he was beyond tired.

March 2, 1945—247 men buried.

January 5, 1945
Hawaii

G AGE HAD LANDED IN PEARL HARBOR the previous month. This was where the Transient Center was located, the center he was assigned to while awaiting orders for his permanent duty station.

It was there he learned the normal tour of duty for a Marine chaplain was 18 months. This would take him until June 1946. He didn't know where he would be; only that it would be as a Marine and would encompass the next 18 months of his life.

Being from the Northeast, Hawaii was quite a different experience for him. There was green everywhere with the numerous palm trees and the beautiful tropical plants in full bloom. It didn't seem like January to him. He wanted to take advantage of every free moment he had to explore the islands, for he did not know how long he would be there. Orders could come down at any time for the next operation.

He went swimming in Waikiki Beach, enjoying the warmth of the water and the majestic grandeur of Diamond Head. There was no scenery like this in New England.

He travelled the coast road with two others in a jeep, seeing all kinds of beautiful and breathtaking scenery. The road followed the seashore all around the island. At points, the mountains would rise up for a thousand feet on the inland side of the road. Then they were surrounded on both sides of the road by miles of pineapple fields as they got close to Schofield Barracks.

A story went around the camp that one could not spend $50.00 a month in Hawaii. Gage decided to put this to the test. On this day he became the liberty-happy chaplain. He started off the morning with $43.00 in his wallet, and went off to test the theory. He started in the Transient Center picking up a pair of Marine dungarees and another khaki garrison cap. Then he went to the Officers Club for lunch, which consisted of a turkey club sandwich and a coke. At the PX he purchased some airmail stationary and some magazines.

He hopped on a bus with his packages and went to Honolulu. He made the round of bookstores and bought a pocket edition of Shakespeare and some back numbers of *Omnibook* and *Coronet*. He then bought more air mail stationery. He was near a 5 and 10, so he went in and ordered a banana split with all the fixings. This set him back 15 cents. When he finished his midday snack, he went back to the ship, as his arms were getting tired carrying all he had purchased.

When he got back to Honolulu, the stores were closing, so he went to Waikiki for dinner at the Moana Hotel. He wanted a steak, but there was no steak on the menu, so he settled for a seafood feast. Dinner set him back $1.50. After dinner he took in the movie *Our Hearts Were Young and Gay*." After the movie he went back to his barracks and found he had only spent $15.00.

That night he wrote in his diary "I am convinced that you can't possibly spend $50.00 a month out here!"

MARCH 1945

NO END IN SIGHT

March 3, 1945 — 68 men buried.
March 4, 1945 — 76 men buried.
March 5, 1945 — 69 men buried.
March 6, 1945 — 146 men buried.
March 7, 1945 — 35 men buried.

September 1944
Closing the First Chapter

AGE PASSED HIS FINAL physical and was sworn in as a Navy Chaplain. In typical military fashion, he was issued orders to report to the Navy Chaplain School in Williamsburg, Virginia, in four days.

As thrilled as he was, he knew there was more work to be done than could be accomplished in the allotted time. All their furniture was stored in Springfield, and Dell was allowed to stay in the parsonage for a few extra weeks to tend to the moving and cleaning out the house. They decided Dell would take Billy and move back to Albany with her parents. The future was certainly cloudy for the young family.

He had mixed emotions leaving the Palmer church. It was his first parish and as is the case in most of life's endeavors, the memory of the first anything would always be special. In the past year the church had an average attendance of 243 people. This was a large increase from the 103 that had attended during his first few months back in 1940.

The previous church calendar year, which ended in May, was a complete financial success. All the bills were paid and there was a surplus of $642.00. The contributions to current expenses were up 25 percent from the previous year, while contributions to missions showed a 50 percent increase over the previous year.

The treasurer's report had pleased Gage, for it was not merely a record of receipts and expenditures, but an amazing record of the loyalty of the church people, his flock.

He wrote in his diary he was proud to boast that Palmer was "the best little church in the Northern Baptist Convention." This was no idle boast to Gage. For four years he had the wholehearted support of the congregation. The cooperation they showed each other and the spirit of harmony they worked together in made him feel very lucky. He sensed their loyalty to the church and to him.

For a young minister's first parish, this was certainly an ideal situation. There would always be a special fondness for the little church in Palmer.

MARCH 1945
WHAT PRICE VICTORY?

March 8, 1945 — 40 men buried.
March 9, 1945 — 56 men buried.
March 10, 1945 — 75 men buried.
March 11, 1945 — 40 men buried.
March 12, 1945 — 150 men buried.

JANUARY 27, 1945
BOUND FOR IWO JIMA

THE CONVOY LEFT Honolulu Harbor for a journey across the Pacific Ocean to a small island named Iwo Jima. The Marines were informed of their next island to conquer in a briefing the day before.

Iwo Jima was an important mission and was assigned to the Third, Fourth and Fifth Marine Divisions, veterans from prior island campaigns against the Japanese.

The importance of taking Iwo was spelled out to the Marines. It was an island located halfway between Saipan and Japan. Beginning in November of 1944, our B-29 Superfortress bombers were bombing Japan from the islands of Saipan and Guam. This was a 1600 mile flight one way for these planes. The bombers had the capability to fly a longer range than fighter support planes could fly. The fighters had to turn back well before the island of Iwo, so Japanese fighter planes could harass the B-29s without fear of confronting fighter escorts.

To counter this, the B-29s flew at an altitude between 20,000 and 30,000 feet, a height the Japanese fighters could not reach. This seriously hampered the success of the bombing campaign. Bombers were more effective at 5,000 feet, but it was imperative to have fighter escorts at this level to protect the B-29s.

Iwo had two airfields built with a third runway under construction. These airfields were now home for many Japanese fighters that patrolled the air looking for American bombers making runs to Japan. Many bombers experienced engine trouble from the long flight or were hit by anti-aircraft fire over Japan. This would force many of them to fly at lower altitudes, thus coming under attack by enemy fighters. Whether shot down or forced to ditch into the water, the ocean was vast and chances for survival weren't good. Many airmen were killed, drowned, captured or eaten by sharks. The choices weren't good.

The high command decided the island needed to be secured to stop the enemy fighters from creating havoc for the bombers. Securing Iwo also meant the airfields could be used by American fighter planes as a base so they could escort bombers to Japan and back. The island would become a floating aircraft carrier for fighter escorts.

During the briefing, the men were informed that numerous casualties were expected, perhaps more than any previous invasion. Intelligence estimated there were some 13,000 Japanese soldiers on Iwo and the island was very heavily fortified with all kinds of guns, pillboxes and bunkers.

Iwo was also considered Japanese soil. The Japanese had mined sulfur from the island and had small communities built there to support the mining industry. Therefore, this would be the first assault on Japanese territory. It was not expected to be easy.

As the convoy headed west across the water, Gage wrote in his diary: *To say I am dreading combat is to put it mildly. Even the doctors who have been with the 4th Division in other operations say this is going to be worse than any of the previous invasions. So I try to think of everything else I can except the operation, and I have so many plans for our post-war happiness, if, if . . .*

MARCH 13, 1945
MARKERS

THE CEMETERIES WERE ADORNED with new objects. Grave markers were installed on each grave. These markers were white wooden crosses with names on each cross of the dead service member interred at that grave.

Gage watched as hundreds of Marines walked through the cemetery reading names on the crosses. It was a procession of haggard and tired looking Marines. These were not the Marines of recruitment posters, all clean and sharply dressed. These were Marines of unkempt and filthy uniforms. Marines with shirts unbuttoned, pants hanging outside of their boots and their heads bared of helmets or caps. Marines that had no intention of passing any silly inspection. They were there to pay respects to their fallen brethren. They had been through hell together and now they came to say goodbye and in many cases, thanks.

Gage watched as they slowly walked up and down each row. Many knelt before markers with their heads bowed.

When others saw them in this position, they paused and waited for their fellow Marine to stand up and move before they walked past. Everyone was paying their respects and allowing others the same regard. There was no pushing or shoving, or much noise for that matter. It was a solemn occasion and it went on for much of the day.

There was still work to do. Even though men had filled the cemetery rows where the white crosses had been erected, there were holes being dug for new burials. Gage's heart was heavy for each of those boys kneeling down with bowed heads, but he could only console them from afar. He had his own work to carry on with.

Send some comfort their way, Lord.

Gage was informed that someone from G-2 Photo Section was coming out to take pictures of a committal service. It would be for the division files only and not released for any public use. Gage would get a copy or two for himself as a memento.

March 13, 1945 — 100 men buried.
March 14, 1945 — 55 men buried.
March 15, 1945 — 27 men buried.

Committal Service

March 15, 1945
Diary entry

Let it never be said that a man becomes a chaplain for selfish reasons. Even though they pay me $300 a month, I would gladly trade it for the chance to sit in at Billy's first birthday today.

Chaplains on Iwo Jima
March 1945

FEBRUARY 18, 1945

T HE FLEET WAS IN PLACE. The boys were tying up loose ends. Tomorrow was D-Day. Hundreds of Marines would hit the beach and encounter . . . what? No one knew for sure. Everyone was lost in their own thoughts.

There were two Protestant services scheduled—one in the morning and one in the afternoon. Gage presided over the morning service, while Chaplain Sneary gave the sermon. There were roughly 300 present on deck for this service. Communion was offered at the end of the service.

In the afternoon, Gage would be doing the preaching. He spent much of midday pondering what he would say. He had never been in combat, but now he was responsible for speaking some words that for many would be the last sermon they might ever hear. He felt quite inadequate for this role, yet it was thrust upon him.

These boys who would be hitting the beach tomorrow had more to fear than he did. They needed words of encouragement and assurance. He berated himself for feelings of inferiority and went to work, preparing his sermon.

He took out his small red book of *Psalms* and thumbed through them, reading different ones to find the right tone. He would read the first verse, and if it was not what he was looking for, he would then seek another psalm to read. He did this a few times until he came across *Psalm 27*. The first verse grabbed him and he read more:

> *The Lord is my light and my salvation: whom shall I fear? The Lord is the strength of my life: of whom shall I be afraid?*
>
> *2. When the wicked, even mine enemies and my foes, came upon me to eat up my flesh, they stumbled and fell.*
>
> *3. Though a host should encamp against me, my heart shall not fear: though war should rise against me, in this I will be confident.*
>
> *4. One thing have I desired of the Lord, that will I seek after: that I may dwell in the house of the Lord all the days of my life, to behold the beauty of the Lord, and to inquire in his temple.*

When he was finished reading this psalm, calmness came over him. He was ready to prepare his sermon.

The afternoon service began. Gage looked over the crowd and estimated about 200 present. Chaplain Vierling opened the service and handled all but the sermon. Gage stepped up to preach.

He opened with a pictorial description of St. Paul walking to his death. Paul was the first Christian to make an amphibious landing in Europe and he went through the same kind of hardships these men were facing. There were two main points of emphasis in his sermon and Gage delivered them with deliberateness.

The first point was thus: an amphibious landing tests a man's courage to the very limit. The second point followed: an amphibious landing tests his faith to the limit.

He noticed the boys listening very carefully and he sensed his words had grabbed them. He could only hope so.

That night at dinner, he was treated to his first last supper before combat. Everyone dined on tenderloin steak with all the fixings and ice cream for dessert. It was the best feast he had had on board ship. How ironic it should be saved for the last night.

March 16, 1945

Dedication of the 4th Marine Division Cemetery

Iwo Jima
March 16, 1945

My Dearest Sweetheart:
Yesterday was a solemn day. There were at least 4,000 Marines of the 4th Division lined up around the cemetery long before the hour of dedication. They stood for many minutes in the hot sun without a sign of emotion and without saying a word to their buddies. It was as though they were in some great cathedral where every stone and every pew was sacred. Nearly a half hour before the ceremony the general arrived, and all stood at attention as he came into the cemetery. They watched him as he greeted the

corps commander, the C. O.'s of the other divisions, and the various members of his staff. They saw him take in the whole cemetery with a long, swift glance. They said to themselves, 'These are your men, General, your men who died for you. Yes, but these are also our buddies who died for us. We knew them back in camp. We went through P. I. with them. We saw them molded into fighting Marines at Lejeune. Then we followed them overseas and watched them climb the cliffs and storm the pillboxes and man the guns. And we saw them die as mortar after mortar crashed with that sickening, crunching sound among them. Yes, general, they are your men, but they are our men too.'

Then at last it was time for the dedication ceremony to start. It was short, far too short to pay the tribute the dead deserved. The Marine Corps hymn and 'Rock of Ages' was played by the band, an invocation by the Jewish chaplain, a few words by the division chaplain, the general's remarks, and the benediction by the Catholic chaplain. Then came the solemn moment, however, when the three volley salute was fired followed by the playing of taps. Then we all snapped to attention as the flag was raised above the cemetery and the National Anthem was played. It stirred up all the emotions in me that had been suppressed during the strain of the last three and a half weeks, and I felt the tears trickle down my cheeks.

The cemetery looks beautiful now. Three weeks ago it looked hopeless. We were attempting to set it up on a hillside above the beach where the soil was nothing but shifting volcanic silt. It took a bulldozer nearly three days to scoop out a level trench in order that the men might be laid in there. Meanwhile, the bodies piled up outside until at one time there were nearly 400 lying within 50 yards of my foxhole. Still, life had to go on, and we ate three meals a day and we slept at night in the midst of that stench. Eventually, we got them all buried, and then the bulldozers scooped the earth back into the trench, and the trucks brought in real dirt and packed it down on top of the volcanic sand. Then the markers were put up, the graves were mounded, a stone fence was placed around the cemetery and painted white, and a flagpole raised at one end with the Marine Corps emblem in white stones around the flagpole. On this side of the cemetery is a small plot where the war dogs are buried. The 3rd Division cemetery is right next to ours, but the 5th Division set theirs up on the other side of the island.

One of the doctors said the other day that this has been the 'healthiest' island that our men have ever fought on in the Pacific, in that no one has been sick and there have been no epidemics of any kind. But in the hospital, they have had at least one major operation to perform every hour of the day and night, as the men have been brought in with every kind of wound in the book, and some that were not in the book.

Word that our men were just taken off the front lines this morning reached us a few moments ago. Yet the island was officially declared 'secure' two days ago. It was secure, however, in name only, as our men have been fighting just as desperately for these last two days. Anyhow, that means that if we can get the bodies of all the men killed during the last forty-eight hours and bury them today, our work at the cemetery will be almost done. The only thing left to do will be to put up the remaining markers. Then we can pack up and go aboard ship, surely a most pleasant thought.

In the last week or ten days, I have read hundreds of letters written by the wives and sweethearts of the men, for they make up a large part of the personal effects which come to us. Never before have we had as many married men with children killed as we have had this time. This indicates that they were men who were drafted this past year, most of them being about my age, having been deferred several times until finally they could be deferred no longer. It is one of the saddest things I know that war should do this to people, to take the heads of families and send them off to die, leaving thousands of little children to grow up without any daddies. But for the grace of God and the fact that I am a chaplain instead of a fighting man, I, too, might be lying out there right now.

If and when we go into combat again, would you include in your letters the news about our division as you get it back home. That is one of the things all of us want to know. We have seen what goes on out here, so we want to know how much of it is reported to you at home, in the way of casualties, etc. As a matter of fact, some of the fellows have received clippings from their home town papers about the progress of the battle, and it is passed around from hand to hand very eagerly. From some of the letters I have read in personal effects, I got the impression that the true reports of the battle were held up at *first. One wife wrote to her husband on February 22nd that steady progress was being made, and the invasion was reported as ahead of schedule, although there were some three thousand casualties already. Another one wrote that it was reported that this battle was not as tough as Tarawa. It sort of made me wonder how long it was before the true reports started coming in to you folks back home.*

Now I guess I'll knock off for chow. It has been a wonderful hour that I have spent with you, and I send you all my love and all the kisses you can imagine. You are always my constant inspiration, and every hour of the day you're in my thoughts. So all of my love and prayers go with this letter.

Always, your favorite chaplain,

Gage

MARCH 17, 1945
JOURNAL ENTRY ON IWO JIMA

We had our final committal services today making a total of 1800 men buried in the 4th Division cemetery. Of the officers who were on the same ship with me on the way out, we have buried at least 10. One of the men in our small fellowship group is also lying in the cemetery. It was as though he were one of the boys from our own parish, for I had grown to look upon the boys of that fellowship group as my very own.

The majority of men we buried were killed by shrapnel rather than bullets. Shrapnel has terrific force and literally tears a man to pieces, leaving gaping holes in the head or arms or legs or belly, or else tearing them off completely. Some of the men we buried were not even identifiable, as they had been so torn to pieces that there were only 15 to 20 pounds of body left and it was buried in a cardboard box. When the bodies were first collected, I did not go any nearer to them than was necessary, but as the division wanted a count each day on the number of bodies, I was asked to count them about 4 every afternoon. The first week it necessitated walking among row after row of unburied men who had died with the greatest possible violence, and counting them accurately. At first, the only way I could do it was to hold my nose and smoke one cigarette after another. But day after day of living under such conditions soon changed that until I could walk among them with hardly a thought of how unbearable it was.There was a team of 5 men who registered each man before he was buried. They removed all personal effects and determined the cause of death. Then the ditty bags containing the personal effects were brought to the burial officer (Lew Nutting) who went over them with his assistant (Gus Sonnenberg) and myself. We looked them over very carefully, and made an inventory of each one. Then a tag was put on the outside of the ditty bag and it was handed over to the personal effect officer (Jack Greeno). He had to pack them in a big box and when we get back to camp, he will have to go over each one carefully, and send them to the Marine Corps Commandant in Washington.

Most of the boys had wallets and pictures of their loved ones, and it was always heartbreaking to see a picture of a wife and child, which happened again and again.

Most of them also wore I.D. bracelets, quite a large number a ring of some sort. A smaller number had wrist watches, then there were other things such as cigarette cases, lighters, religious medals and rosaries and new testaments.

We had to remove "art" pictures from their wallets, and also pictures of the Marines taken with girls in Honolulu. In addition, we had to remove a large amount of more or less filthy literature that the boys carried.

Once in awhile, we ran across something funny which provided a little humor in the midst of an otherwise humorless task. For example, there was one cartoon which showed a group of women Marines in boot camp, nude to the waist, lined up for inspection. The male officer who comes out to inspect them says: "Good grief! I said KIT inspection!"

March 19, 1945

Back on Ship

GAGE WAS THRILLED to be back on board ship. He had been on Iwo for 26 days, during which he had not had his clothes off once. He wanted to be clean.

He stripped down and stepped into a hot shower. The water poured over him, washing away the accumulated dirt and grime. He stood transfixed by the water, letting it cleanse his body and reach down into the deep crevices of his soul for a thorough steam cleaning. It was as a baptism to him. He had survived.

He had been through one hell of a storm, many times feeling that hand on his shoulder and many times not. His thoughts were jumbled by all that he saw, all that he experienced and all that was beyond his comprehension. Would he be able to write any of this down? Would he be able to fully share what he went through? He had no answers, just the steady flow of water gently welcoming him back to life.

MARCH 20, 1945

March 20, 1945

Dearest darling of mine:

I have been amazed at the amount of mail that has come through at Iwo Jima. Altogether I have had 30 letters from you and 19 from Mother. Of course, there has been nothing but first class mail, so all papers and magazines and packages are back at camp, so I reckon I'll have plenty to look at when I get back, don't you think?

This may be a gruesome letter in some respects, but I want to record my experiences in detail while they are still fresh in my memory. That will help you to understand better what I have gone through and the changes that have taken place. Censorship naturally forbids the revealing of certain information, but since I can write fully of my own experiences, that is the most important thing both to me and to you.

Well, the fighting is over, and the Army has relieved us, coming in with large garrison forces. I talked to an army chaplain on Saturday who expects to be here at least a year. That is not a very pleasant prospect, and he doesn't relish it at all. Thank goodness we don't have to stay on indefinitely. While there have been no air raids since our fighter planes arrived, I expect there will be plenty later on, unless the Japanese air power has been knocked out more than we think.

I have been reading an article written in Coronet especially for the G.I. wives in which it is emphasized that no man who goes overseas to combat comes back exactly the same. It goes on further to point out that the success of war marriages depends almost 100 percent on the wife's ability to adjust to her soldier husband. In normal times, it should of course be a 50-50 proposition. But these are not normal times.

I, too, will not come back the same person that I was when I left four months age, and neither will your three brothers, Emory, Bob and Bill. Last night I spent a couple of hours thinking it through, and it came to me that there were at least three ways in which I have changed so far. First, until I left to come overseas, I had always felt a sense of inferiority and inadequacy in my parish work at Palmer because I felt so young and inexperienced. Now the very fact that I have come overseas, been with the Marines in combat, and in the toughest battle the Marines ever fought, has changed all of that. Don't mistake me. It has not made me cocky or egotistic, but never again will I have that same feeling of inferiority or inadequacy or inexperience. After 18 months of dealing with men of all types out here, I feel sure I shall come back to parish work with an entirely new outlook, and with an eager desire to be more helpful to my people than ever before. The very fact that when I first went to Palmer, the thought of having to make parish calls constantly was almost a terrifying thing indicates the way that feelings of inexperience reacted on me. I expect that after this war such a thing as making a parish call will be a very pleasant duty after some of the things I have gone through. Yes, darling, there is absolutely no vicarious way to get this experience.

In the second place, as you well know, I had certain preconceived and very definite notions as to the way a minister and a minister's wife should act in a parish.

At chaplains' school, we also were given certain definite ideas as to procedure a chaplain should follow. But when you get out in actual service, you throw overboard a lot of the ideas you got in chaplain school, and you use your own common sense. Now I can see how much wiser I would have been had I acted that same way in Palmer! But the tradition of a minister's life and my background as a youngster in a personage was so strong that it clung to me like an octopus, despite all of your good intentions to rescue me from the evil monster and turn a minister into a human being!

I trust that I have learned that lesson, and that you will find me very human when I get back, not once in a while, but always, and that the rule of common sense will apply to all our actions. I don't think I will ever have occasion again to tell you what a minister's wife should do. You have been very patient in spite of my inadequacies, and I am sure that so far as the human equation is concerned, you were a much better minister's wife than I was a minister!

In the third place, my life at Palmer was marked by the fact that my work was my master instead of me being the master of it. I had heard of so many stories of ministers who did not do any systematic studying after they left the seminary, and their preaching grew dull and stagnant accordingly. So I was determined not to let that happen to me. What I did not realize was the possibility of biting off more than I could chew, which is exactly what happened. The result you know only too well.

I think I told you even before I came overseas that I was never going to hold myself down to such a rigid schedule again. I shall study, yes. I shall read, yes. But I shall balance it with a steady diet of romance, friendship and ecstasy with you. So that our post-war life together will be a continuation of the fun we had together at Newton. How's that? I am eagerly looking forward to an evening of playing cards with you, of dancing with you, of listening to music with you, and of doing all the other things you always wanted me to do with you!

Yes, my darling, those are the three ways in which I have changed so far. But there is something else which has matured me even more and given me a deeper and newer kind of faith. It goes back to the sermon I preached at Chaplains School the day before I received orders. In that sermon, I spoke of Phillips Brooks, who wanted to be a teacher, but who failed and became a minister instead. That was not his first choice, but his second choice. It was as though he wanted sea duty, I said, but got stuck with shore duty. Then the next day I got my appointment: "HEADQUARTERS, FLEET MARINE FORCE, PACIFIC."

It was a real, first class test for me. I wanted shore duty, and I was getting stuck with the hardest kind of duty any Navy chaplain ever gets, duty with the Marines. It was a terrifying thought from the very start. I felt sick about it at first. Why should this happen to me? Why should I be the only one in my class to be sent overseas directly to the Marines? I was full of resentment, disgust, and disillusionment. But gradually I began to see that if I could make the best of it and triumph, I would never be afraid of life again, for there could never be anything worse than this which could happen to me.

The fact is, of course, that the mental agonies I suffered from the day I received my orders until we finally landed on Iwo were a great deal worse than the actual agonies of ducking into foxholes to escape sniper fire or mortar shells, worse than the terrors of the air raids of the first week, worse than the smell of death that was ever present, and worse than the sights of hundreds upon hundreds of dead Marines. I can say it now that I died a thousand possible deaths before we ever landed on Iwo Jima! I faced all the possibilities in my own mind, so that the real thing was less terrifying than it might have been.

If I indeed triumphed over my despair, as it looks to me now, I can take anything that is handed to me from now on with stoic calmness.

As soon as we hit the beach, I saw the first dead bodies. They were Marines killed before they had taken a dozen steps. They had all fallen forward and lay there on the sand still clutching their rifles and their packs still on their backs.

Robert Sherrod says in Time that these were the most horribly mangled bodies he has ever seen in the Pacific War.

I was asked to count the bodies about 4 every afternoon. I found I could only do this smoking one cigarette after another to ward off the horrible stench.

Soon, my duties included gathering the belongings off the dead Marines. This was quite challenging at first, but eventually I reached the point where I could turn a dead man over, or pull things out of his pocket, or cut off his dog tag, or almost any other thing that was needed, and then if I lifted up my hand and found it covered with a man's guts or his brains, I calmly brushed it off in the sand, and when I got a chance later on, washed my hands with soap.

One of the colonels told me the other day that he had sympathized with me for three weeks. Oh, I said, my job wasn't so bad, and somebody had to do it. For three weeks I have been sympathizing with the men in the front lines.

The other day I saw one of the officers on our ship. He had been in the 30th Replacements and had graduated in the same class with Emory. [Dell's brother]

I had talked with him on the ship about Emory. Like Emory, his job on this operation was supposed to be merely unloading supplies on the beach. But at the end of the first week, the casualties were so heavy that the replacements were ordered up into the lines. This officer, whose name was Sinclair, was walking through the cemetery looking at the markers. He had just come back from the front. With a three weeks' growth of beard on his face, I hardly recognized him. His eyes were terribly sunken from weariness and lack of sleep. He had aged many years in those three terrible weeks, and I said to myself, here's what Emory might have looked like had he been through this!

I, too, have aged, but in a much different way from those who had to fight at the front. Now I am a man in more ways than one, and I hope that someday I will be the kind of man of whom you will be terribly proud.

So long for now, my precious darling. I'll write you another long letter later about my experiences of the first week, and about the personal effects we took off bodies.

My love to all, and all my love to you, with a hug for Billy, and millions of kisses for you.

Always, your favorite chaplain,
Gage

March 1945

Dedication by Another

WHEN THE 5TH MARINE DIVISION cemetery was being dedicated, a Jewish chaplain from New York City by the name of Roland B. Gittelsohn was one of the speakers. Excerpts from his speech appear in many books about the battle of Iwo Jima. The following excerpt comes from the book *The U. S. Marines on Iwo Jima by Five Official Marine Combat Writers.*

This is perhaps the grimmest, and surely the holiest task we have faced since D-Day. Here, before you lie the bodies of comrades and friends. Men who until yesterday or last week laughed with us, joked with us, trained with us. Men who were on the same ships with us, and went over the sides with us as we prepared to hit the beaches of this island. Men who fought with us and feared with us. Somewhere in this plot of ground there may lie the man who could have discovered the cure for cancer. Under one of these Christian crosses, or beneath a Jewish Star of David, there may now rest a man who was destined to be a great prophet— to find the way, perhaps, for all to live in plenty, with poverty and hardship for none. Now they lie here silently in this sacred soil, and we gather to consecrate this earth in their memory.

It is not easy to do so. Some of us have buried our closest friends here. We saw these men killed before our very eyes. Any one of us might have died in their places. Indeed, some of us are alive and breathing at this very moment only because men who lie here beneath us had the courage and strength to give their lives for ours. To speak in memory of such men as these is not easy. Of them too can be said with utter truth: "The world will little note, nor long remember what we say here. It can never forget what they did here."

No, our poor power of speech can add nothing to what these men and the other dead who are not here have already done. All that we even hope to do is follow their example. To show the same selfless courage in peace that they did in war. To swear that by the grace of God and the stubborn strength and power of human will, their sons and ours shall never suffer these pains again. These men have done their job well. They have paid the ghastly price of freedom. If that freedom be once again lost, as it was after the last war, the unforgivable blame will be ours, not theirs. So it is we the living who are here to be dedicated and consecrated.

Too much blood has gone into this soil for us to let it lie barren. Too much pain and heartache have fertilized the earth on which we stand. We here solemnly swear: This shall not be in vain! Out of this, and from the suffering and sorrow of those who mourn this, will come—we promise—the birth of a new freedom for the sons of men everywhere.

These are pertinent words that still speak to us from across the ages.

Afterword

I N HIS AFTER BATTLE REPORT, Admiral Chester Nimitz wrote these words concerning the men who fought on Iwo Jima; "Uncommon Valor was a Common Virtue."

Iwo Jima was the only battle in the Pacific where the Marines suffered more casualties than the Japanese. Official records show 5,931 Marines were killed with the total number of casualties at 25,851. This is just the number reported for the Marines. All U.S. forces that participated in the battle show 6,821 killed with casualties numbering 28,868. It is evident that the Marines suffered the highest percentage of the casualties. Japanese forces were estimated at around 20,000. By the end of the battle only 1,083 were taken as prisoners.

The airfields became important in the air campaign against Japan, until the end of the war. More than 850 B-29's were saved from having to ditch in the ocean, by being able to land at Iwo. This saved the lives of all the crewmen on these planes.

Lt. (j.g.) Gage Hotaling never again experienced combat during his stay in the service. He was mustered out in April of 1946, after serving his full tour of duty. When he returned home, wedding vows were renewed with Dell, who was his earthly inspiration in coping with all the death and destruction he witnessed on Iwo Jima.

During the Korean War he was called back into active duty with the Navy. This eighteen month tour was spent at a base in Bainbridge, Maryland. This was his last call to active duty.

Gage spent his life as a parish minister in American Baptist churches in Massachusetts. He always wanted to be in the trenches with the people he served. His pastorates included churches in Hyannis, Needham and Springfield. The churches in Needham and Springfield had expansive building projects under his watch.

He retired from full time preaching in 1985 at the age of 70, but continued as an interim minister or supply pastor until his death in 2010.

He was the last living chaplain who participated in the battle of Iwo Jima, but he attributed this to the fact he just lived longer than the others.

As with anyone who lives a long life, heartache did not spare him or Dell. Bill, their oldest son, died tragically in 1970 at the age of 26. As tough as this was, it did not affect their faith. I am sure it gave him a more empathetic approach when helping parish members deal with tragic death of loved ones.

His calling into the ministry was a voice that told him to finish his father's work. He never sought the limelight for himself, only the opportunity to serve others as their pastor in the service of God. He preached over 4,000 sermons and selflessly ministered to the many parishioners of his churches.

Until the day he died, he received newspapers from the towns of every church he served in, sending sympathy or congratulation cards to any relative of members of his former churches.

In 1995 a new monument was dedicated in Newington, Connecticut, by the Iwo Jima survivors association, spearheaded by a spunky retired dentist, who fought on Iwo and who would not take no for an answer. This dentist's name was George Gentile. He was told he was crazy for attempting this scheme.

This park and monument was built entirely with private donations. No government money was used. The monument is of the six flag raisers, and it sits on Route 9 in the Iwo Jima Park. The names of the 100 dead service members from the state of Connecticut adorn the front of this monument.

Gage was there on that day when the monument and park were dedicated on February 23, 1995,

50 years after the battle. George would not be deterred or denied. Yet, when George spoke, he knew the Iwo Jima Living Memorial was for those brave heroes who did not come home. He was honoring his fallen brethren. This was his tribute to them. It was not for himself.

At that ceremony Gage was asked to open with a prayer. These were his words:

Almighty God, our Heavenly Father, in whose hands are the living and the dead, we have gathered here today for the dedication of this Memorial Statue to honor our comrades who gave their lives in the service of our country at Iwo Jima.

We know that you are not only a God who has been our help in ages past and are our hope for years to come, and so we pray today that we may have assurance of your abiding and continuing presence.

We are here today because we served our country 50 years ago when we left our homes and loved ones. Many of us have been in combat and know what it is to face the enemy.

Many of us have crouched in foxholes and seen enemy planes attacking us. Many of us have crawled into our helmets and tried to make ourselves as small as possible. And all of us remember the shouting and cheering and celebrating when the news came that the war was over and peace had come at last.

We will never forget those who did not come back, who gave the last full measure of devotion to the cause of freedom.

And now, O God, we pray that you will inspire us by their memory, encourage us by the comradeship of those who walk with us, and consecrate us to the task of those who come after us, until the day dawns when we shall have everlasting peace.

This we ask in the name of the Prince of Peace.

Amen.

Every Memorial Day and Veteran's Day there was a service at the Monument, and many survivors attended each year. George Gentile always convened over the ceremony until his death. James Boyle led us in patriotic songs and Gage Hotaling delivered the opening prayer and benediction.

George always had outside speakers, and one year James Bradley, author of the book *Flags of Our Fathers* spoke. I have his autograph in my hardcover copy of his book. He and I are both sons of Iwo Jima survivors.

George Gentile was not content with just one monument. He wished to put up a monument to honor the medical personnel and the chaplains. George discovered a picture of Gage doing a committal service and called Gage to ask if this picture could be depicted on the monument. Gage was proud to have his picture be carved into this monument. This was the picture taken on March 13, 1945, on Iwo Jima.

Looking back at the date in his journal we find these words: *"The G-2 Photo Section took a picture of me holding a committal service today. It is mainly for the division files, as it will not be released, but I'll have a copy or two for myself."*

Fifty-five years later on Veteran's Day in the year 2000, that picture was unveiled and dedicated on a monument honoring the work chaplains did during combat. It stands next to the monument honoring the medics in the Iwo Jima Living Memorial Park in Newington, Connecticut. I am sure this was one of the proudest moments of his life. He would gladly take pictures with people who asked, but he never stood there boasting it was his likeness on the monument. For a man who spent his life in service to others, this is a most fitting tribute.

I took him to see the movies *Flags of Our Fathers*, and *Letters From Iwo Jima*. He proudly wore his Iwo Jima survivors hat to both movies and was thanked for his service by numerous people in the theater.

I remember one quote about these movies that he uttered. After seeing Letters From Iwo Jima, he sat in the theater staring at the stage and said after the credits ended, "The Japanese were just as scared and terrified as we were." Then he just shook his head. I guess this thought had never occurred to him.

Dell, Gage and Kerry Hotaling at Survivors Monument

COMMENDATION

COMMENDATION
FOR
LIEUTENANT (jg) (ChC) EDGAR GAGE HOTALING
(408687)

For service set forth in the following Citation
"For meritorious performance of professional duties as a chaplain attached to Headquarters Battalion of a Marine Division, from 19 February to 16 March, 1945, during operations against the enemy in IWO JIMA, VOLCANO ISLANDS. Lieutenant (jg) HOTALING served with the Graves Registration Section of the Division. For two weeks, at the start of the battle, those engaged in work at the cemetery were subjected to enemy mortar and artillery fire. During this time, and in spite of enemy fire, he assiduously devoted himself to the rendering of proper, dignified religious rites in the burial of men of all faiths. His devotion to duty served as an inspiration to all who were engaged in the mentally trying task

of burying the dead. His devotion to duty and his untiring efforts were instrumental in maintaining a high level of morale among those who worked with him. His conduct throughout was in keeping with the highest traditions of the United States Naval Service."

C. B. Cates
Major General, United States Marine Corps
Commanding Fourth Marine Division

WORDS INSCRIBED ON THE MONUMENT

CHAPLAINS RESTORED OUR SPIRIT AND FAITH IN THE DARKEST HOURS OF COMBAT AND CONSOLED AND PRAYED WITH THE DYING AS THEY MADE THE ULTIMATE SACRIFICE FOR THEIR COUNTRY.

IWO JIMA SURVIVORS ACKNOWLEDGE WITH GRATITUDE THE BRAVE AND COURAGEOUS SERVICE BY THE CHAPLAINS TO US OUR COMRADES AND OUR COUNTRY.

OF THE 50 CHAPLAINS IN COMBAT UNITS AT IWO JIMA:
3 CHAPLAINS WERE WOUNDED.
6 WERE AWARDED BRONZE STARS.
MANY OTHERS RECEIVED LETTERS OF COMMENDATION.

Gage Hotaling

THE COST OF FREEDOM

The following letters were written from Chaplain Hotaling to grieving parents or spouses of fallen servicemen. I have not included any names or addresses, just the content of the letters to show more of his work while on duty during World War II. All the letters had the same heading:

CHAPLAIN'S OFFICE
HEADQUARTERS, FOURTH MARINE DIVISION, FMF
c/o FLEET POST OFFICE, SAN FRANCISCO, CA.

27 April 1945
Dear Mr. xxxxx:
May I convey to you my sincerest sympathy on the loss of your son, who gave his life so bravely on the shores of Iwo Jima. As his chaplain, his death was a matter of personal sorrow to me as well as to his buddies. Since he had been with the 4th division for a long time, he had made many friends, and was always considered a very good leader. He had been awarded a Letter of Commendation for his fine work on Tinian, and everyone who knew him realized that no man deserved

such an award more than he did, for it was a real tribute to his outstanding leadership and ability.

I am sure that your son did not want to die any more than the other gallant marines who made the supreme sacrifice on Iwo Jima. But every one of them realized the price that had to be paid for the kind of freedom that we cherish. Now he has given the last full measure of devotion, and I can assure you that he was buried with full military and religious rites. You will find enclosed with this letter a copy of the memorial service held at the time of the dedication of the cemetery on Iwo Jima.

May you be comforted in the knowledge that your son gave his life so that others might live, and may the peace of God that passeth all understanding be with you through these dark days.

Very sincerely yours,
E. G. HOTALING
Chaplain, USNR

This response was hand written.

June 3, 1945
Chaplain E. G. Hotaling USNR
Dear Sir:

Mrs. xxxxx and I wish to express our appreciation of your letter of sympathy on the loss of our son Sgt. xxxx. He often spoke of attending church while in the service and I know he appreciated the privilege of doing so.

He had not mentioned the Letter of Commendation for his work on Tinian. Suppose it is with his personal effects, but have not received them as yet. Would like to have a copy of it if possible to put in my memory book.

It is very hard to become reconciled to the loss of a son. Nevertheless, we are proud of his good record both at home and in the service of his country and all our memories of him are only the pleasantest.

Once again, Mrs. xxxxx and I want to thank you for whatever help and guidance you may have been to our son in his last days and may God guide and assist you in carrying on the good work that we know you are doing.

Sincerely yours,

March 22, 1945
Dear Chaplain Hotaling,

I've been wondering how to go about a certain matter and last evening I read an article in the paper about your job on Iwo Jima and thought you may be able to tell me. I'll start from the beginning as near as I know how and try not to take up too much of your time.

My fiancé was killed on Iwo on the 23rd of Feb. From what I understand you actually send a picture of the grave home to the family and we're expecting that, but if possible I'd like to learn a little something about his last days. I know you are the busiest man in the outfit and I thought maybe some buddy would maybe write. My boyfriend was Cpl. Xxxxx, a B.A.R. man in (Co, Bn and Div omitted from this text)). What makes it harder I haven't his serial number. He was a veteran of Namur, Saipan and Tinian, being wounded on both Saipan and Tinian. While at his rest camp before going to Iwo, he was also on the football team there that I believe made quite a name for itself in the Pacific.

I don't know what more information I can give you that would help. I would not bother you with this, but he never told me the full name of many of his buddies and I don't know how to get in touch with any of them. There was one fellow he wrote about a number of times, a fellow named Sal, that's all he ever said. They seemed inseparable and I know that Sal was in his squad and aboard ship with him before the invasion. I would very much like to get in touch with him if it is all possible. If you could help me it would be greatly appreciated by myself and his family. I know even if you can't help you'd like to so I can understand.

I do want to say that if at any time, now or in the future months, if there is any little way I could help you or any man in the 4th Div. I would be more than glad to do so. Whether it was by writing to someone or sending something they might need or anything at all, I'd be glad to correspond with anyone who may want a letter, also, as I know what letters can do for morale.

If this is not enough information then maybe I could send along some pictures. If you can help me I'll be very grateful and if not, why I want you to know that I am grateful for the fact that you are there helping those men and every other chaplain in the service. Everyone back here feels that the chaplains are personal friends and the job you do is tremendous.

Thank you, Chaplain Hotaling, for letting me take up these moments of your valuable time and I hope and pray that soon you and all those boys can return to a peaceful country.

A Friend

CHAPLAIN'S OFFICE
HEADQUARTERS, FOURTH MARINE   DIVISION, FMF
c/o FLEET POST OFFICE, SAN FRANCISCO, CA.
18 April 1945

Dear Miss xxxxx:
Your letter of 22 March was here when I arrived back from Iwo Jima. May I convey to you my sincerest sympathy on the loss of your fiancé, Cpl. xxxxx, who gave his life so bravely on that field of battle.

Since I did not know Cpl. xxxxx personally, I have turned your letter over to the chaplain of his regiment. As soon as possible, he will answer it and endeavor to give you whatever information he can. Meanwhile, I can assure you that he was buried with full military and religious rites. May you be comforted in the knowledge that he gave his life so that others might live.

Very truly yours,

E. G. HOTALING
Chaplain, USNR

CHAPLAIN'S OFFICE
HEADQUARTERS, FOURTH MARINE DIVISION,
FMF
c/o FLEET POST OFFICE, SAN FRANCISCO, CA.

18 June 1945

Dear Mr. xxxxx:

Your letter of 3 June is at hand requesting information concerning the death and personal effects of your son, Sgt. Xxxxx. I have communicated with the Tank Battalion office, and also with the Division Personal Effects Officer, and will give you what information I have been able to obtain.

Your son's buddy, Sgt. Xxxxx, tells me that xxxxx was killed on Iwo Jima on D-Day about 10 in the morning. He was a gunner in a tank that was hit shortly after the attack on the beach had begun. In trying to get away from the tank, he was killed instantly by a direct hit of a mortar shell. Sgt. xxxxx is planning to write to you and you will probably receive a letter from him soon, and he will give you more details about xxxxx's experiences in combat and in rest camp.

The following personal effects were taken from his body on Iwo Jima: a wallet containing $3.00, a check for $1.00, and 51 pictures; also a wristwatch, a pen, and a cigarette lighter. A few articles of clothing were also found among his personal effects in camp. These were all sent some time ago to Marine Corps Headquarters in Washington. In due time they will be shipped to his wife, because she was listed as next of kin at the time of his death. However, since she has moved and they are now divorced, you may receive them at your address under her name. I would suggest, therefore, that since she is now divorced, and you are next of kin, that you keep the personal effects when they arrive.

Memorial services for Protestant boys of headquarters and tank Battalions killed on Iwo were held in our camp on Sunday, the 27th of May, and I enclose a copy of that service with this letter. May I extend my sincerest sympathy in your great loss.

E. G. HOTALING
Chaplain, USNR

Here was their hand written response.

June 24, 1945
Dear Chaplain,
We received your welcome letter of June 18 and I am writing to thank you for the information about our son Sgt. xxxxx. We appreciate what you have done for us and we ask God's blessings to be with you in such a worthy cause and that you will be guided by the Holy Spirit to keep those that are in your care in the Holy Way. I think that's a wonderful mission just to preach to our boys and remind them of their duties toward

God and the hopes of eternal life. I will close thanking you again. Lots of love and good wishes.

Yours very truly

Mr. + Mrs. xxxxx.

Chaplain Hotaling also wrote letters of condolences to people from his parish or from the church he served in while attending seminary. These letters were not part of his official duties as a naval chaplain, but part of his duty as a minister of God to his people, his humanity to his fellow men.

CHAPLAIN'S OFFICE

HEADQUARTERS, FOURTH MARINE DIVISION, FMF

c/o FLEET POST OFFICE, SAN FRANCISCO, CA.

18 April 1945

My Dear xxxxx:

One of the first things I learned upon my return from Iwo Jima was the news of your husband's death in Germany. While I did not know xxxxx personally, yet he does not seem like a stranger to me. I have known many Bobs and Bills and Toms and Harrys out here who have come from every section of the country. I have seen the pictures of their wives and children, and I have seen the proud look on their faces as they have told me their plans for the future. Then, they have said with a note of hesitancy, if something happens and we don't come back, our wives will carry on for the sake of our children. That's what we want them to do and we pray that they will do it bravely and courageously.

Xxxxx was not killed on Iwo Jima, but more than four thousand men with similar hopes and ambitions laid down their lives on that rocky soil. It was my duty to bury nearly one half of those men, and my heart cried out bitterly that such things had to happen, that so many men would never see their wives and children again. Then I realized that just as long as tyranny and oppression exist in the world, some must die in order that others might live.

No, xxxxx, your husband did not want to die, any more than did these gallant marines on Iwo Jima. But every one of them realized the price that had to be paid for the kind of freedom that we cherish. Now he has made the supreme sacrifice, and he wants you to help him prove he did not die in vain. How can you do that? By facing a lonely future as bravely and courageously as you can, by giving your child the very best training possible, and by instilling in her the great American ideals. But most of all, by keeping his memory alive in her life. For that is a part of xxxxx that will never die.

It will not be easy to smile through these dark days, but I believe you can do it, for that is what he would want you to do. Always remember, too, that his love surrounds you forever. May you be comforted by these thoughts.

Her handwritten note follows:

June 18, 1945
Dear Gage,

It was quite some time ago that I received your letter of sympathy, and words of comfort. I have read your letter many times, trying to make myself do and realize what you wrote to me in such an understanding way. It is hard, Gage. I feel that God has given me a cross too hard, and heavy to bear. I know that it is God's strength that I have existed on these past 6 ½ months, as I have no strength or will of my own. I do realize that God is making me live without the one whom I love most, to take care of our baby. As you said, Gage, it is a very lonesome life, but you give me credit which I do not deserve, as I am not brave or courageous. I cannot seem to get hold of myself, and find it very hard, sometimes impossible to meet people. I had all the faith in the world that my husband would come home. This shock is so very hard to bear and believe.

I am sorry, Gage, you did not know my husband. He was a wonderful person and a perfect husband. We were completely happy and devoted, and had a beautiful life together. I am glad I am his wife, and so much a part of him.

I have learnt recently that he had been through one of the hardest battles of the European war. He was on guard duty in a newly captured town in Germany, when he was instantly killed by a German sniper. These words are very hard to write, but so much harder to believe. He didn't suffer. He was too good to suffer.

Time now is the only thing that will help me get strong again, to be able to bear my cross. I am doctoring for my health, but as my doctor said, only time and God can help to heal my heart and mind. I will probably gain physically, and be better able to face this world alone, but I shall never forget.

We have a little girl, Gage, who is the image of her wonderful daddy. I hope I can bring her up to be a credit to him, and make of her all that he would want her to be.

You have been through a great deal, Gage, and your duty a hard one. We, your friends are proud of you, and we know God will bless you. Thank you for writing to me, Gage. I have many questions in my troubled mind, some of which you seemed to have answered in your appreciated letter. For you and the many others God has spared, may this war soon end, and return you to your loved-ones waiting for you here at home.

Sincerely,

xxxxx

CHAPLAIN'S OFFICE
HEADQUARTERS, FOURTH MARINE DIVISION,
FMF
c/o FLEET POST OFFICE, SAN FRANCISCO, CA.

8 June 1945
My dear xxxxx and xxxxx:

I have just heard the tragic news about your son. I wish I could see you personally, but since I cannot, this letter conveys my feelings to you. Nothing I can say or do will bring xxxxx back to you, but I want you to know how deeply I share this sorrow with you.

I have sat here at my desk reminiscing and there are so many things about xxxxx that come to mind. I remember the first time I met him on the Sunday I began my ministry at Palmer which was also the Sunday that his dad started teaching in the Sunday School. I taught the class that xxxxx (son) was in that Sunday, and when he told me his name, I asked him if he was related to xxxxx (father). He replied. "That's my pop!" How proudly he uttered those words, and somehow I never forgot them. Then I remember the first time I visited your house and how xxxxx showed me his room. It was full of the things that boys like, and his room was an eloquent testimony to the fact that he was a "regular fellar." I remember another time when Dell and I spent an evening with you three and we played ping pong on the dining room table, and how much fun we had. And then I remember how quickly he grew up, and the day we had dinner with you just before he left for training and how we wished him Godspeed that day. And the letters he wrote to the Service Committee were unique, for they were written in his own inimitable style. Yes, xxxxx had a large place in my heart and it is boys like him who are helping to keep our country free in this time of crisis.

I went in to the service just about a year to the day after he did, so I have had nine months so far to work with men. I went from Chaplains School directly into combat at Iwo Jima, where it was my sad duty to bury nearly two thousand men. My heart cried out bitterly that such things had to happen, that so many men would never see their homes and their loved ones again. Then I realized that just as long as tyranny and oppression exist in the world, some must die in order that others might live.

While xxxxx did not give his life on the field of combat, nevertheless he died while in the service of his country. He knew, therefore, the price that had to be paid for the kind of freedom that we cherish. He would, I am sure, have been willing to make the supreme sacrifice if he had been called upon to man a gun against the enemy.

These will be dark days for you, for you are now sharing in the greatest sacrifice any parents ever make. You have given your only son to his country. No words of gratitude the government will ever utter can completely repay you for your loss. Only your faith in a living God can give you the comfort and strength to carry on during the long days ahead. May the peace that passeth all understanding be with you now and forevermore.

Most sincerely,

E. GAGE HOTALING
Chaplain, USNR

About the Author

Kerry Hotaling is a member of the Friends of Gettysburg and the Civil War Trust. He has published two books on the battle of Gettysburg. This is his first venture into World War II. He is a land surveyor in Western Massachusetts and during the winter months he can be found curling. He lives with his wife in western Massachusetts.

Other Books by Kerry Hotaling

What They Endured, What they Wrought:
Comparing Regimental Casualties
at the Battle of Gettysburg

When you visit the Gettysburg battlefield, you are surrounded by numerous regimental monuments. These were erected in the 1880's and 90's, by survivors of the battle to honor their fallen brethren. This book is a small history of some of these regiments and how they fared at the battle. It is the story of the ten highest regiments in the killed in action and percentage loss category. It can be used by the first time visitor or the seasoned Gettysburg sojourner. Stand by these monuments, open this book and descend into the maelstrom that was the battle of Gettysburg.

The Yankees Had Something to Do With It

"The Yankees had something to do with it," is a quote attributed to General George Pickett when asked after the Civil War why the Confederate Army was defeated at the Battle of Gettysburg. This book brings the reader onto the battlefield and into the strategy sessions during the Gettysburg Campaign from the viewpoint of several Union generals that "had something to do with it"! Experience the campaign as it unfolded for these men. General Doubleday, General Hancock, General Warren and General Meade are a few of the characters who bring the story of Gettysburg to life.

CPSIA information can be obtained at www.ICGtesting.com
Printed in the USA
BVOW05s0448230216

437703BV00005B/12/P